"Jeffrey Cohen's work is a worthy, lively and instructive version of these ancient and ineffable poems. The easily accessible register of language, conveyed in probably the only poetic form known to those whom the author seeks to reach, is greatly effective. Overall, he succeeds in reproducing the flow and integrity of the Hebrew original and, in the case of obscure and difficult verses in the Hebrew (and there are many), his judgment is remarkably consistent with up-to-date research. It is clear that he has made extensive use of many versions, ancient and modern. While his Psalms naturally maintain a proper and delicate Jewish flavour, that in no way precludes their use by Christians."

Rev Dr Andrew Macintosh (from the Foreword)

"You really do a most impressive job on these difficult texts, combining sound renderings with literary polish and exegetical allusion."

Professor Stefan Reif, Former Professor of Hebrew and Director of The Taylor-Schechter Genizah Unit, Cambridge University

"Every new translation of a classic text affords us a fresh perspective on the power and beauty of the original. In this striking and wonderfully accessible translation of the Book of Psalms, Rabbi Dr Jeffrey Cohen gives us renewed insight into the greatest of all books of religious poetry, the unsurpassed music of the soul as it sings its songs to God."

Rabbi Lord Jonathan Sacks, former Chief Rabbi of Great Britain

"I can see why they impress, and they would make an attractive volume."

Professor Nathan MacDonald, University Lecturer in Hebrew Bible, University of Cambridge

"So much in the poems is arresting and impressive, and the overall sense is of a faithful, and yet innovative, rendering. Your translations frequently give a new twist to familiar texts, and quite a few are downright brilliant! One is reminded that the psalms are for adaptation and contemporising, and that the evidence for this begins in the Psalter itself. A superb anthology of engaging and imaginative re-phrasings of the Psalter seems in prospect. One greatly looks forward!"

Robert P. Gordon Emeritus Regius Professor of Hebrew, St Catharine's College, University of Cambridge.

"One of my retirement projects is an attempt to get to know the Psalms. As I work my way through them I look at various translations as well as the original Hebrew text. Your version in many passages is blisteringly original and immensely topical. I look forward keenly to reading the Jeffrey Cohen Psalter when it appears."

Philip Skelker, Former Headmaster, Immanuel College, Bushey, and English Master, Eton College.

"Thank you so much for the privilege of pre-viewing your magnum opus. As a 'man in the pew', I mumble the psalms, only occasionally taking on board their import. However, when I read through your version I realised that there is no comparison with any previous edition. You have created a new form which touches the emotions directly. I know that one needs to study to fully appreciate the majesty of the psalms, but, magically, you seem to have brought the text to life in a way that goes straight to the heart. Please excuse this gushing praise but I have been very moved!"

Dr Maurice Faigenblum, Stanmore, Middlesex, UK.

The Book of Psalms

The Book of Psalms

Poetry in Poetry

Jeffrey M. Cohen

Foreword by A. A. Macintosh

WIPF & STOCK · Eugene, Oregon

THE BOOK OF PSALMS
Poetry in Poetry

Wipf & Stock
An Imprint of Wipf and Stock Publishers
199 W. 8th Ave., Suite 3
Eugene, OR 97401

www.wipfandstock.com

PAPERBACK ISBN: 978-1-5326-5076-5
HARDCOVER ISBN: 978-1-5326-5077-2
EBOOK ISBN: 978-1-5326-5078-9

Manufactured in the U.S.A.

For Gloria,

Wife, friend and inspiration.
A truly worthy woman who can find? Her value far exceeds that of the most precious gems. She is the source of her husband's confidence, ensuring none of his endeavours fail (Proverbs 31:1-2).

Contents

Foreword

THE PSALMS OF ANCIENT Israel, of Judaism and of Christianity, constitute one of the most translated texts in history. Written originally in Hebrew in the first millennium BCE, they were known to early Christians only in the Greek translation until, in 400 CE, it dawned on Jerome that the Hebrew text was the original, prompting him to set about translating anew the Hebrew text into Latin. In the Jewish tradition there were Aramaic translations known *as Targums*, and it is supposed that they grew out of oral renderings offered by synagogue interpreters following the formal reading of each verse in Hebrew. The *Targums* are, perhaps naturally, free and replete with explanatory material.

Motivation and intention lie behind all translations. The Jewish Scholar Aquila (117-138 CE) was primarily concerned to force his Greek translation to reveal as much of the original Hebrew as possible, creating thereby perhaps the most literal translation known to us. By contrast, Jerome's intention was rather to convey the sense of the original, and this in the elegant Latin of his day. He was also keen to improve the accuracy of the translation as compared with that of the previous Latin translations from the Greek, defined by their nature as textual 'grandsons.'

Where English translations are concerned, that of Miles Coverdale, done in 1538, has been widely loved for some 400 years. His version, however, made from the old (pre-Jerome) Latin version, which in turn was a rendering of the Greek, has the characteristics of the Curate's Egg. In places the version offers the beauty of Shakespearian English; elsewhere, being a textual 'great-grandson' of the Hebrew, it lapses into sheer, if beautiful, nonsense. Impressive for its scholarly accuracy and its incorporation of up-to-date research into the ancient Hebrew language, is *The Cambridge*

Liturgical Psalter, commission by the Church of England in the 1970s. It is a completely new version of the original Hebrew in modern English.

Against this vast and complicated background, Dr Jeffrey Cohen has crafted his own English translation of the Hebrew. He seeks to present the Psalms in very simple, straightforward, contemporary English, under-standable, he hopes, by contemporaries and by the young. The words of his version are moulded into a consistent pattern of rhyming verse. In the interest of sustaining this pattern, additional lines are deployed (in italics) which do not answer to any words of the original Hebrew. These additions are consistent with the surrounding material and may be characterised as like the (Aramaic) *Targums* of early Judaism. Jeffrey Cohen is no new Aquila. Rather, his style is in the Jerome tradition, but emphasized greatly, since his clear desire to convey the sense of every verse is normative.

I have not had time carefully to work through more than the first sixty of his psalms, but it is enough to conclude that it is a worthy, lively and in-structive version of these ancient and ineffable poems. The easily accessible register of language, conveyed in probably the only poetic form known to those whom the author seeks to reach, is greatly effective. Overall, Cohen succeeds in reproducing the flow and integrity of the Hebrew original and, in the case of obscure and difficult verses in the Hebrew (and there are many), his judgment is remarkably consistent with up-to-date research. It is clear that he has made extensive use of many versions, ancient and mod-ern, and the details are set out in his own Introduction.

Cohen's Psalms naturally maintain a proper and delicate Jewish fla-vour. But that in no way precludes their use by Christians. The high esteem in which Jerusalem, the Temple and its cult is held is easily spiritualized in the universally based prayers and aspirations of Christians. There is St. Paul's "Jerusalem which is above, the Mother of us all", and there is the ar-gument of the Epistle to the Hebrews. The reference to and study of Israelite Kingship (as indicated by the Psalms) is important evidence for Christians regarding definitions of the person and nature of Jesus of Nazareth.

The intimate and plain language of this work probably suggests pri-vate, rather than public or liturgical use. That does not preclude its use in sermons or other occasions of religious instruction.

There is no doubting Dr Jeffrey Cohen's love of and devotion to the Psalms of David.

A.A. Macintosh

Acknowledgments

THIS RENDERING OF THE Book of Psalms is the culmination of a lifetime's exposure to its lyrical beauty and eloquence of expression, its incomparably moving, faith-inspiring and spiritually-energizing aura, as well as its most urgent summons to pursue the highest standards of religious, ethical and moral conduct. Selections from it have inspired and accompanied me for over seventy years in the context of my daily and festival prayers. It was when I went to theological College and launched myself into what was to become a lifetime's study of biblical texts and scholarship that I began to appreciate the variety, perplexity and depth of the psalms and to grapple with the many problems associated with the attempt to reconstruct their respective backgrounds and life-situations. For that I owe an eternal debt to my early teachers— notably, Mr Eli Cashdan and Professor Naphtali Wieder— for providing me with the necessary academic tools that have stimulated my literary creativity over the decades. As a lecturer at The University of Glasgow (1970-1980) I was further enriched and encouraged by my doctoral supervisor, the head of the Department of Hebrew, Professor John Macdonald, and by my fellow lecturer, Dr (later Regius Professor of Hebrew at Cambridge University) Robert P. Gordon.

My fellow undergraduate student (and Best Man), Stefan Reif, later Director of the Cambridge Genizah Research Unit and Professor of Medieval Hebrew Studies, has remained a cherished friend and a reservoir of knowledge and advice. I would like to place on record my special thanks to him for his encouragement of and faith in this project and for having commended it to his fellow academics in Cambridge. In this context, my sincere appreciation is extended to Robert Gordon, Nathan Macdonald (Reader in the Interpretation of the Old Testament and lecturer in Theology, St John's College) and Andrew A. Macintosh (Dean of Chapel and

Director of Studies in Theology, St John's College), and to Rabbi Lord Jonathan Sacks. I would especially like to thank Dr Macintosh who, together with his former student, Rev Dr Cindy Eagle, subjected many of my psalms to critical assessment, giving me the benefit of their literary and scholarly observations. Sincere appreciation is also extended to Mr Philip Skelker, former teacher of English at Eton College and Head Teacher at King David School, Liverpool and Immanuel College, Bushey, UK., for proof-reading my pre-submission version and for many helpful suggestions. Thanks are also extended to the editorial team at Wipf & Stock, and particularly to Matthew Wimer and Ben Dieter, for their advice, patience and meticulous attention to detail.

No words can express the extent of my indebtedness to my wife, Gloria, who has lovingly tolerated my air of distraction throughout the decades of my studies, researches and publications, and who has been such an active and supportive pastoral partner in my various congregational ministries. The pleasure we have derived from our children, Harvey, Suzanne and Keith, Judith and Bob, Lewis and Suzanne, and our fourteen grandchildren, has also been the motivation for a life of contentment, gratitude to God, and peace of mind, which in turn served as a stimulus to my spiritual, literary and academic pursuits.

Introduction

The Problem of Translation

THE SCHOLARLY AND LITERARY endorsements of this work (see p. i–ii) provide an indication of the originality and pursuit of accuracy that has been my priority in this rendering of the biblical Book of Psalms into rhymed verse. It also provides corroboration of the fact that, although I profess the Jewish faith, my approach has been entirely non-denominational.

Rather than simply using one or more of the standard English translations as a basis for my poetic version, I have gone back to the original Hebrew text, analyzing every word and phrase in the light of the ancient, medieval and modern translations and commentaries which have been the starting points for my own interpretation.

The problem of translating this collection from the original Hebrew is that it is not always possible to determine precisely what the psalmist had in mind, or, in many instances, how the thought-process proceeds from one line or stanza to the next. Translators and commentators frequently confess this difficulty which is exacerbated by the fact that there are many words that occur only once in the Hebrew Bible (*hapax legomena*), and have to be guessed at from their context or inferred from similar words occurring in one of the cognate Semitic languages. This may be demonstrated at a glance with reference to the Bible edition of *The Jewish Publication Society* (Philadelphia, PA, 2000), which supplies brief footnotes listing every Hebrew rendering wherein "the meaning of the Hebrew is uncertain." In the case of the Book of Psalms it lists no fewer than 106 words or phrases where that uncertainty is manifest!

The translator cannot conveniently omit such problematic words or phrases, although some editions do precisely that! Any serious attempt at elucidation has not only to fit the immediate context but has also to be tenable semantically, either in relation to the three-letter root-meaning of the problematic Hebrew word or phrase, or as a derivative of a cognate Semitic language.

A further difficulty is posed by the necessity to render into English, or any other foreign language, an idiomatic expression in the original Hebrew. This is not only due to cultural, linguistic or geographical differences between the respective languages, resulting in the fact that no corresponding idiomatic expression may exists in the target language, but also because, "The meaning of many idioms results from the figurative extension of the original situation which is often unknown to most speakers" (See, Ghusoon Subhi Khalil, www. *Problems of translating idioms from foreign languages*, page 3; accessed 20/8/2017). Thus, any attempt to translate an idiom literally will prove either nonsensical or incomprehensible in most cases.

J. H. Breasted appositely refers to a problem encountered by translators attempting to provide an accurate version of the New Testament for the tribes of Alaska. When they sought to render the term 'Good Shepherd' they were stymied by the fact that those tribes had never seen a sheep or encountered the notion of a shepherd! (Breasted, *Ancient Records of Egypt: Historical Documents*, 1. Chicago, Illinois, USA: The University of Chicago Press, 1906. Preface, ix.) Thus, because the psalms are replete with idiomatic expressions, translators are obliged to resort to a measure of paraphrase if they wish to convey accurately to their readers the essence of the psalmist's original intention and frame of mind. It was only after completing this work and confronting this problem that I read the introduction to *The Cambridge Liturgical Psalter* (Aquila Books, Cambridge, 2012), whose editors sought to provide "a liturgy for public recitation and singing"— an objective not unrelated to that of providing a rhymed verse rendering.

Not surprisingly, they faced the identical problems of how to translate idiomatic Hebrew expressions and how to resolve the differences in length of lines between the two languages. The solution they describe in their introduction served precisely as my own guide:

> On occasion, to give singers sufficient syllables to sing, we have
> added one or two words to a half-verse, but these have always been
> justifiable expansions of the meaning of the Hebrew.

The editors also admit that for the same reason they did not consistently employ the terms 'God' and 'Lord', and

> have sometimes added an explanatory word, or offered a paraphrase
> or a double translation, to convey the full meaning in English.

Such an approach is even more necessary when facing the extra challenge of attempting to render the original into rhymed verse. Throughout this work I have struggled to employ paraphrase sparingly, though I remain optimistic that the general reader will be content to sacrifice literalness for the goal of creating a version that can stand on its own as a meditative and inspirational manual, conveying the joy, thanksgiving, fear or pathos, that invest the individual psalms, and the mood or situation of the psalmist as he gave poetic expression to his deepest feelings.

As a prelude to deciding on each rendering I consulted the main ancient versions (The Aramaic *Targum*, the Greek *Septuagint* and the Latin *Vulgate*), a wide variety of Hebrew and English commentaries, standard English translations, such as *The Authorized Version, Revised Standard Version, New English Bible*, etc., and some modern translations and commentaries, such as Berlin, Adele and Marc Zvi Brettler, eds. *The Jewish Study Bible*. Oxford, UK: Oxford University Press, 2004; Parrish, V. Steven. *A Story of the Psalms: Conversation, Canon and Congregation*. Collegeville, Minnesota: Order of Saint Benedict, 2003; Alter, Robert. *The Book of Psalms*. New York/London: W. W. Norton & Co., 2007; Frost, David L., John Emerton, Andrew Macintosh, *et al.*, eds. *The Cambridge Liturgical Psalter*. Cambridge, UK: Aquila Books, 2012.

THE PSALM-HEADINGS

The above difficulties are compounded when it comes to the issues of author attribution in the headings of some of the psalms as well as elucidation of some enigmatic references within the psalm-headings. Other than in the case of sixteen psalms, all are endowed with some superscription which seeks to provide information regarding either the putative author of the psalm, the occasion for which it was composed, its literary type, its melody, the musical instrument that should accompany it, or its liturgical use in the Temple. In some instances, the heading consists of a phrase which appears to be no more than the title of a popular hymn to which the psalm was to be sung. That these headings were not original but appended by some later editors or Temple musical directors may be inferred from the fact that in the Greek version of the Septuagint (third-century BCE) a substantial number of the psalms are endowed with totally different headings.

It is generally assumed that the term *lam'natze'ah*, which occurs in fifty-five of the psalm-headings (and for which we have followed the rendering, 'For the Director'), refers to that particular musical director or choir master; and it is not inconceivable that the personal names of the individual maestros—which were subsequently omitted at the final redaction of the Book of Psalms—may have been inserted, following the term *lam'natze'ah*, at the top of their personal copies of the psalms they had selected to be included in the services they directed. Some scholars take the view that these particular *lam'natze'ah* psalms—"The Directors' Psalter"—constituted the prayer book of the synagogue in the Greek period (Brown, Francis, S. R. Driver, Charles A Briggs, *A Hebrew and English Lexicon of the Old Testament*. Oxford, UK: Oxford University Press, 1907, 664a).

The final editor of the Book of Psalms would have made his choice from among the collections housed in the Temple repository; and that eclectic nature of the book explains why we encounter considerable duplication of ideas, phrases and verses, often within the same psalm.

I have made no attempt to 'rush in where angels feared to tread,' by attempting to elucidate those abstruse psalm-headings, but have contented myself with merely transliterating the words as they appear. Similarly, I have entirely omitted inclusion of the word *selah*, notwithstanding that it occurs over seventy times in the Psalter. Various suggestions have been offered to explain the term, such as that it represents a musical notation indicating a place in the psalm at which the Temple choristers were instructed to raise their voices to crescendo. This connects the term to the Hebrew root *s-l-l*, 'to lift up,' from which the noun *sullam*, 'a ladder,' is derived. A Greek tradition, on the other hand, renders it as *diapsalma*, 'a musical interlude,' possibly suggesting a time for pause and reflection.

Other Hebrew headings that recur frequently are *Mizmor*, *Mikhtam* and *Maskil*. Although the noun *zimrah* (*'melody; song of praise'*), from the same root as *mizmor*, occurs a few times outside of the Book of Psalms (Ex 15:2; Is 12:2, 51:3; Am 5:23), the noun *mizmor*, found over fifty times in Psalms, curiously occurs nowhere else in the entire Bible. The popular rendering, 'psalm,' is derived from the Greek *psalmos*, a term whose basic meaning is, 'to pluck with the fingers,' and was applied to the creation of music on the harp. While this term is used to refer to any song sung in religious worship, it is to the contents of the Book of Psalms that this term is generally applied, with the name 'hymn' being used more generically to describe the former.

The noun *Mikhtam* occurs as a designation of Pss 16 and 56—60. Although its precise meaning is unknown, a popular explanation associates it with the noun *ketem*, 'fine gold', viewing it as a tribute to the superior quality of that psalm.

The name *Maskil* is applied to thirteen psalms: 32, 42, 44, 45, 52-55, 74, 78, 88, 89 and 142. It clearly derives from the root *s-kh-l*, meaning, 'to instruct, be prudent, make wise', though it is difficult to sustain that nuance in relation to all the psalms to which it is applied. The verb is also found in the sense of 'to be skilful', especially in the context of playing music (See II Chr 30:21-22); and this might suggest that the *Maskil*-psalms were sung to the accompaniment of a musical composition that was regarded as complex or difficult to play.

A less common heading is *Al ha-gittith* which is found in the heading of Pss 8, 81 and 84. Many scholars explain the term in relation to the word *Gat*, the name of the Philistine city, Gath, and assume that the psalm-heading represents an instruction that it should be sung to the accompaniment of the harp produced in that city. Others connect it with another meaning of the word *gat*, namely 'a vine-press', and suggest that it was a psalm that was popularly sung to the accompaniment of the wine production.

The heading *Lehazkir* occurs only twice (Pss 38 and 70), and is also unclear. Its literal meaning is 'to remember' or 'for a memorial', and may be a recommendation that the psalm be committed to memory as efficacious in time of need. Another suggestion was that the term implies that the psalm was written in order that God might *remember* the petitioner favourably. This is supported by the occurrence of the term *askarah*, 'a memorial', in the context of the meal offering (Lev 2:2), where it appears to have had that same sense, that the offering would have the beneficial effect of God '*remembering* the petitioner favorably'.

Some of the psalm-headings include a reference to the event which inspired the original composition, such as, "A psalm of David, when he fled from before Absalom his son" (Ps 3); "A psalm. A song at the dedication of the house (Temple?)": Ps 30); "A psalm of David when he feigned madness in the presence of Abimelekh who threw him out and he left" (Ps 34); and, "A Maskil of David when the Ziphites came and told Saul, 'Know that David is hiding among us'"(Ps 54).

A poignant heading is *Al muth la-ben,* "On the death of a son" (Ps 9). Such a dirge-like melody would certainly suit the content of the latter psalm which contains such sentiments as, "He does not ignore the cry of the afflicted; He who requites bloodshed is mindful of them" (v 13), and, "Have mercy on me, Lord . . . You who lift me from the gates of death" (v 14). The heading *(Al) Alamoth* (Ps 46) is probably a combination of the words *Al* and *muth.*

More frequently among the psalm-headings we find a brief Hebrew phrase that seems to make little contextual sense, such as *Al shoshan-nim . . . Shir yedidoth,* literally, "On the lilies . . . A love song" (Ps 45). While in the latter case such a heading might be justified as an expression of the love and admiration felt by his subjects for the king, that sense could not be sustained for the other psalms that bear that same heading (Pss 60, 69 and 80). Ps 69, for example, is an out-pouring of unremitting anguish as the psalmist stares death in the face. A common view is that such abstruse phrases in the psalm-headings represent rather an allusion to the title of a popular song of the day, to the tune of which the psalm was to be sung. This would appear to be the case with the phrase *Al ayyelet ha-shahar* ("Deer of the Dawn": Ps 22), which, otherwise, seems to bear no association to the theme of the psalm. The heading *Al tash'heth* ("Do not destroy") of Pss 57—59, on the other hand, seems most appropriate to their content wherein the psalmist cries out at a time of crisis. It is understandable therefore that they would have been recommended to be sung to a melody that echoed that precise mood.

Other headings are believed to refer to the musical instruments to be used as accompaniment to the singing of those psalms. We have referred above to *Al ha-gittith.* In this category are the terms *Al ha-nehiloth* (Ps 5), perhaps derived from the noun *halil,* 'a pipe' or 'flute'; *Al ha-sh'minith* (Pss 6 and 12), literally 'On the Eight', and possibly a reference to the eight-stringed harp.

The precise sense of the heading *Al mahalath* (Pss 53 and 88), is difficult to determine as its root, *h-l-h,* has three unconnected meanings, 'to be sick', 'to appease or entreat', and 'to adorn'. The ancient Greek versions of Aquila and Symmachus (second-century CE) render it as 'For the dance', which assumes a variant reading of the original Hebrew, namely *Al me-holoth,* from the noun *mahol,* 'a dance.' The mood and contents of both psalms makes it extremely unlikely, however, that such psalms would have been accompanied by dancing!

We turn now to a group of fifteen psalms (120—134) that bear the superscription *Shir ha-maʾaloth*, literally, "A song of ascents." The precise sense of the term is unclear, but the common view is that these were psalms recited or sung by pilgrims when wending their way 'up' to Jerusalem for the three main pilgrim festivals of Passover, Pentecost and Tabernacles. However, although many of the psalms in this section are consistent with that setting, exuding a joyful spirit and a sense of profound pride in the beauty of Zion, six of them (Pss 120, 121, 123, 124, 130 and 131) make no reference to Zion or Jerusalem, or to the House of God as a reference to the Temple. Their theme is rather that of fear in the face of distress or trial, or, as in the case of Ps 121, an expression of faith and strong conviction that God would come to the psalmist's aid and remove the looming peril. Ps 124, on the other hand, is a thanksgiving for divine aid in having defeated a violent enemy against all odds. It is difficult, therefore, to place those six psalms as a unit within the milieu of the pilgrims' joyful repertoire!

Jewish tradition offers the alternative suggestion that the term *maʾaloth* ('ascents') derives from the fact that each succeeding psalm was sung by the Levitical choir as the priests made their way in procession each day along the fifteen Temple steps. This situation is also mirrored in Christianity wherein the name 'Gradual' (from the word meaning 'step' in Latin) is used to denote material from the Psalms recited as the reader ascends the Altar steps.

In Eastern Christianity those fifteen 'Songs of ascents' are also invested with special significance, and are read at Friday evening Vespers throughout the year. This liturgical borrowing from Judaism goes back to the early days of those respective faiths' parting of the ways. In early Judaism it was the practice of *Hasidim*, members of religious fraternities, to rise at an early hour each day to attend synagogue in time to recite the entire Book of Psalms before the commencement of the morning service. This practice was taken over into early Christianity, although its recitation was spread over the entire week.

These psalms are especially popular in synagogue liturgical tradition. Ps 121 ("I lift up my eyes to the hills; from where will my help come?") and Ps 130 ("Out of the depths I call You, O Lord. Listen to my cry; let Your ears be attentive to my plea for mercy") are both prescribed for recitation by the congregation on behalf of any of its seriously ill members, or in a situation of local peril or national trial. Somewhat curiously—but understandably when we consider that it makes an almost seamless transition from fear to the conviction that God's help and deliverance are at hand—Ps 121 is also the most popular choice for occasions of communal thanksgiving and celebration.

Ps 126, containing the sentiment that "those who sow in tears shall reap with songs of joy" (v 5), namely that, although the farmer may have meagre seed with which to sow, yet a bumper harvest is promised for him (v 6), is employed as the introduction to the Jewish Sabbath and Festival Grace After Meals. And Ps 128, containing the sentiment, "When you enjoy the fruit of your labors, happy and fortunate are you" (v 2), is recited as the closing psalm of the Service for the Conclusion of the Sabbath, as a prelude to the resumption of the working week.

Finally, the *Halleluyah!* collection. These are the ten psalms (106, 111—113, 135, 146—150) which either begin (Pss 111 and 112) or both begin and end (Pss 106, 113, 135, 146-150) with this interjection of praise of God. The early Catholic and Eastern Orthodox Church pronounced the term as *Alleluia*, under the influence of the transliteration found in the Greek Septuagint version of the Psalms. It was used in these traditions in a variety of liturgical ways. In evangelical churches, it is particularly popular as a spontaneous expression of instinctive and powerful spiritual emotion and as an identification with a preacher's affirmation of belief and faith in God.

Few are unfamiliar with the word *Halleluyah!* This is largely due to its popularization by George Frideric Handel who included it as a repeated interjection throughout the climactic chorus to Part II of his most famous Messiah oratorio.

One of the most joyous collections of synagogue hymns, both in ancient Temple times and in Synagogue tradition to the present day, is known as *Hallel* (Pss 113—118). These are psalms of praise and thanksgiving which are sung with great gusto by prayer leader and congregation on all festival days and on *Rosh Hodesh*, the semi-festive occasion marking the appearance of the new moon and the inauguration of a new Jewish month. On Tabernacles, the harvest festival, worshippers wave palm branches in every direction to the accompaniment of the singing of verses from the *Hallel* psalms.

AUTHORSHIP OF THE PSALMS

Individual psalms were certainly composed long before our biblical collection achieved its present form. While both Orthodox Jewish and Christian traditions attribute the authorship of most of the psalms to King David (tenth-century BCE), the early scholars of The Higher Critical School (eighteenth-nineteenth centuries CE) took the view that the psalms could not have been composed before the Judeans returned from exile in Babylon (around 538 BCE), and that most of them were in fact products of the Maccabean era (second-century BCE). This includes those psalms whose headings bear the name of King David.

Such an anachronistic attribution of Davidic authorship could indeed be explained against the background of the Pseudepigraphic Literature (from the Greek, *pseudes*, 'false', and *epigraphe*, 'name' or 'attribution') composed in Judea between the period 300 BCE–300 CE. Many religious writers at that period believed that the most effective way of achieving authority, popularity and wide circulation for their works was to pass them off as having come down from biblical antiquity, and as having been authored by one its illustrious figures. Hence the existence of such works as *The Life of Adam and Eve, The Testament of Adam, The Book of Enoch, The Testament of the Twelve Patriarchs* (purporting to be the dying wishes of Jacob's twelve sons), *The Testament of Moses, etc.* The critical school explained in that same way the other psalm-headings which attribute authorship to Yeduthun, Moses, Solomon, Heman, Sons of Korah, Asaph and Ethan.

⤶

Seventy-three of the psalm-headings contain the Davidic attribution. If we add another two psalms (2 and 95) which the New Testament attributes to David, we arrive at a maximum of seventy–psalms, precisely half the collection, for which that claim was made. A psalm scroll discovered in Qumran attributes a further two psalms (104 and 123) to David, while some scholars took the view that there are a further twenty psalms which, while not bearing the Davidic superscription, yet reflect the circumstances, style, mood and vocabulary of many of the Davidic psalms. This still fell far short, however, of any internal corroboration of the blanket Davidic attribution of authorship of the entire psalter that the Orthodox traditions of both faiths maintained.

It was with J. H. Breasted's discovery and publication of an abundant literature of fourteenth-century BCE Egyptian psalmody at the beginning of the twentieth-century that the scholarly consensus regarding the dating of the psalms was turned on its head. It was now realised just how early Near Eastern psalmody was developed, that it was entirely plausible that the Israelite genre could indeed go back as early as the Davidic period, and that particularly the royal psalms (Pss 2, 18, 20, 21, 45, 72, 101, 110, 132 and 144), which deal with the king's spiritual role in worship, might well be traced back to David himself. This view was supported by such eminent authorities as J. Buttenwieser, J. A. Montgomery and H. Gressman. The fact that the Septuagint (third-century BCE) attributes to David many psalms that do not bear his name in the Hebrew version also suggests that his influence was more widely associated with that genre than is suggested by the Hebrew textual tradition.

THE APPEAL OF THE PSALMS

The Greek version of the Septuagint adds an additional psalm, making a total of one hundred and fifty–one, a Hebrew version of which was discovered in Qumran, while in the biblical Peshitta of some Middle Eastern Syriac churches their psalms were supplemented by a further four psalms. If we factor in the eighteen psalms contained in the Apocryphal work, *The Psalms of Solomon* (first- century BCE), and the contemporary *Hodayoth* (Thanksgiving Psalms) from Qumran, the picture emerges of a genre that won almost universal acceptance as *the* most appropriate source and format for liturgical, petitionary and meditational outpouring. Not surprisingly, the psalms provided the content and inspiration for the Judeo-Christian religious traditions, a popularity that has not waned to the present day.

The issue of their Davidic authorship, whether in whole or part, was mainly of academic concern. It was the mere fact that the ancient custodians of tradition credited King David, accurately or otherwise, with having pioneered that genre that gave it its undeniable spiritual authority and appeal in the eyes of the masses.

The Temple was the divinely ordained house of prayer, so the assumption must have been that King David, who is credited with having designed and laid the foundations for that Temple, would also have been divinely inspired to create its earliest liturgy in the form of the psalms. And that is how they became *the* most cherished source of spiritual inspiration as well as a worthy guide for all of life's vicissitudes. This was largely due to the variety of critical situations that King David had to confront, as chronicled in the Bible and within his psalms, and with which the simple worshipper could identify, and derive succour for his or her own predicament.

While the Five Books of Moses represented the blueprint for the religious way-of-life, the Book of Psalms portrays the struggles faced by people of faith against its many obstacles, notably the evil-doers and the violent who mock and pursue them for their religious integrity, while at the same time serving as a pressure-valve for their own doubts, temptations and inner turmoil. The seemingly arbitrary division of the Psalter into five books would seem to represent a salute to the priority of the Torah and its five books, and may thus point to an understanding of a relationship between the two.

The appeal of the psalms was also due to the comfort that was drawn from their promise of ultimate victory for the pious oppressed, their certainty that goodness would be rewarded with God's grace, and impiety with His censure, and the opportunity that they offered the worshipper to home into, and sing along with, the paeans of praise, joy and thanksgiving as expressed with such beauty and passion by the grateful psalmist. With the introduction of rousing musical and choral accompaniment, the psalmist's own call to "serve God with joy" was amply fulfilled, and the therapeutic value of the psalms considerably enhanced.

This therapeutic dimension was highlighted by John Calvin (sixteenth–century French theologian) when he observed that the Book of Psalms "grants us the permission and freedom to lay open before God those of our infirmities that we would be ashamed to confess before men." Indeed, the psalmist taught the faithful how to address God, what to talk to Him about, how to share their inner thoughts and fears with Him, how to articulate their petitions in an appropriate manner, and, equally important, how to express thanks and gratitude. The Book of Psalms thus made a significant contribution to the cultivation of civility, gentility and refinement within the religious community.

While the biblical and other religious texts offered subject-matter and inspiration for the lessons or sermons in the houses of worship, the Psalter, with the variety of personal, communal and national situations that it chronicled, served, and continues to serve, as the standard resource for religious leaders seeking appropriate hymns for tailoring the liturgy to a wide variety of public occasions.

THE MAIN CATEGORIES OF PSALMS

A debt of gratitude is owed to Hermann Gunkel (1862–1932), the pioneer in identifying the main *gattungen*, or 'categories,' of psalms represented in our Psalter. These include individual complaints or laments, individual psalms of thanksgiving, communal laments and communal thanksgivings. These were later expanded to include enthronement psalms and royal psalms. Since Gunkel, research into psalmody has progressed extensively, and there is much to occupy the interest and attention of scholar, teacher, preacher or popular writer on the subject. The present writer found much inspiration and stimulus in his study of the literature in his far-off student days, in his Ministry, and even more so in his preparation of this work. But it is also the ordinary reader, who employs the psalms for prayer, praise or meditation, who will gain a far greater depth of understanding and a broader perspective of the background of the psalms by familiarizing him- or her–self with the scholarly literature.

Gunkel observed that the individual laments represent the largest category in the Book of Psalms, and that there are, in fact, few thanksgiving psalms. He explained this psychologically, given that human nature is generally quick to petition for needs, but readily forgets to offer thanks or appreciation for benefits bestowed. This could be rationalized, however, on the basis that most people have significantly more difficulties, setbacks and losses in their lives than significant triumphs that call for an instinctive recognition of God's direct intervention on their behalf.

Another charitable explanation for the preponderance of lament is that it is occasioned by the psalmist's strong conviction that God is our true and ready Savior, a reality to which countless individuals in his day —and ever after—have attested through their own experience. As the natural re-action to the many crises of life, the God-directed lament thus represents an affirmation of God's presence and an act of faith and confidence in His redemptive power. As the child instinctively cries out when hurt and in need of the parent's comfort, so do we cry out, complain of our pain, invoke our divine Parent's healing, help and guidance, and express our reliance on Him. The lament is thus a profound and indirect expression of pure faith.

THE METRIC TRADITION IN PSALMS

Translations of psalms into English first made their appearance during the sixteenth-century, and are associated, primarily, with the names of John Daye, Sir Philip Sidney, Margaret Sidney Herbert, Thomas Sternhold and John Hopkins. Metrical psalms were introduced to encourage congregational singing. This was a dramatic departure from original practice wherein singing was the exclusive preserve of the clergy or church choir, or in closed fraternities, by monks and nuns.

The Reformation changed all that; and the establishment of the Anglican Church, with its English liturgy and the *Book of Common Prayer* (1549), demystified the ritual and enabled the masses to participate in the joyful singing of hymns. This, in turn, encouraged gifted theologians, such as John Calvin, to produce metric versions of biblical texts, notably the Psalter, to encourage musical composition and congregational singing, and to generate thereby a more enhanced spiritual joy and emotion. Calvin settled in Strasbourg in 1538, and joined the Huguenot community, to which he introduced *The Genevan Psalter*. This has remained in use by that community and other French-speaking Protestant churches until the present day.

The first complete metric Psalter in English—which also included musical notations—was produced in 1549 by Robert Crowley. He describes his project as "The Psalter of Dauid newely translated into Englysh metre in such sort that it maye the more decently, and wyth more delyte of the mynde, be reade and songe of al men." His English version was followed by editions produced in French (1562), Dutch (1566), and German (1573).

The many challenges inherent in converting the more expansive English prose translations into rhymed verse meant that, in many instances, elegancy of style and accuracy had to be sacrificed, resulting in rather forced renderings. This elicited much criticism from the leading poets of the day, and was taken on board by subsequent writers who moved to liberate themselves from the confines of the translated version and embrace paraphrase, an approach approved by the Church of England.

The trend among versions of the psalms produced during the twentieth-century by English-speaking Reformed churches of the Commonwealth was to move away from paraphrase and return to formulations that were closer to the literal sense of the text. I have chosen rather to steer a middle course and to adhere to the literal sense of the Hebrew original—wherever this was indubitably understood—while avoiding any formulation imposed purely by the necessity of providing a corresponding rhyming word. However, given the variations of the respective Hebrew and English meters, a 'rounding off' of the stanza was required on occasions, through the addition of an extra line or phrase. Where this has been necessary I have attempted to ensure that the added part is consistent with the spirit and sentiment of the context. Furthermore, in order that the reader may readily identify the supplemented words, they have been italicized.

RHYMED VERSE AND ITS CHALLENGES

I have chosen the medium of rhymed verse, notwithstanding its constraints, because of my belief that it best conveys the innate power, lyricism and flowing vitality that infuse the Hebrew original. Its short lines also approximate closest to the conciseness of the Psalter's Hebrew meter, consisting of three or four beats to a line. It is very difficult to capture and sustain that spirit and energy in any prose translation.

As referred to above, a measure of poetic license has been required in facing the challenge of rendering Hebrew psalms into English rhymed verse. This is to compensate for the comparative conciseness of the original Hebrew phraseology, as well as the frequent paucity of English rhyming words available to express the precise nuance of the Hebrew. The same applies in relation to divine names. A characteristic of the psalmist's style is his penchant for invoking a variety of these names (*Adonai* (*YHWH*), *Adonai tzeva'oth, Elohim, El*), often in the context of a single stanza, and, on occasions, within a single line. Clearly, this could not be sustained within the scheme of the short rhyming lines I have employed. Furthermore, whereas most of the standard English prose translations maintain consistency in rendering those Hebrew names as either 'God' or 'The Lord', I did not feel constrained to follow that convention. This is not only because of the insurmountable metric difficulty, but also because it is impossible to sustain any precise distinction in meaning between those individual divine designations as employed in the original Hebrew, just as there is no clear distinction in English between the terms 'The Lord' and 'God.'

The Bible is used in churches and synagogues, and studied in countless universities, theological colleges and homes the world over. This book is intended for them all— scholars and laymen alike—as well as for those who look to the Book of Psalms as a devotional and inspirational manual, a stimulus to faith, and a source for help, guidance and tranquility amid the stresses of modern living. For those more interested in the poetry, it is my hope that they will find inspiration in the work, and appreciate what Professor Stefan Reif has described as its "literary polish and exegetical allusion."

Jeffrey M Cohen

Book 1

Psalm 1

How content is the one
Who has not followed
The advice of the wicked
Who in corruption wallowed;
Who from sinners' ways
Remained aloof;
Spurning those that sit
Beneath cynics' roof;
But embraced God's law
As his total delight
Meditating therein
By day and night.

Like a tree planted
By a gentle stream—
Yielding bounteous fruit
That tastes a dream;
Whose foliage
Is never known to fade—
Is he that aspires
To the highest grade.

Not so the wicked
Who are as short-lived
As chaff which
The wind has sieved;
Hence the final judgment
They'll not survive
And in righteous company
Shall never thrive.

For in the ways of the righteous
God delights;
While evil designs
He speedily blights.

Psalm 2

Why, O why,
Do nations collude
To adopt a hostile
Attitude?
Why do monarchs
And tyrants conspire
Against God and his chosen—
Arousing his ire?
The ropes and chains
They prepare for our neck
We'll sever and smash;
Their plans we'll wreck.

God will mock
Their intrigue;
From heaven
He'll heartily laugh;
Furiously
He'll denounce
That mindless riff-raff.

But I gave allegiance
To my king
On Zion
My holy mount;
And the decree that
God made to me
Let me now recount:
"You are the son
I fathered this day;
Your welfare is paramount.

"As you requested I shall make
Nations your domain;
Your territory shall embrace
The earth's entire terrain.

"With an iron bar
You will crush
All your many foes,
As earthenware
Is shattered beneath
The potter's hammer-blows."

So now you kings
Submit to God
And take this to heart:
World rulers let probity
Set you apart;
The more you tremble
With genuine awe
The more joy
You shall draw.

With pure heart
Offer submission
Lest His wrath aborts
Your God-given mission;
For his flaming anger
Grants no remission
And your goal may be doomed
To perdition.

But if happiness
Be your ambition
Make Him your refuge—
And display contrition.

Psalm 3

A psalm of David
Written in flight
From before his son, Absalom.

Lord, how numerous
Are my foes!
My list of adversaries
Daily grows.

I am made to bear
Their mindless taunt.
"Your God can't save!"—
Is their vehement vaunt.

Yet I know, Lord,
You are my shield;
You raise me up
To a glory
Revealed.

So when
To the Lord
I present my plea,
I am confident
He will answer me
From His holy mount
With alacrity.

Thus, I'll not fear
The myriad foes
In ambush waiting
To deliver their blows;
And when I lie down
Soundly I'll sleep
Knowing God will rouse me

And blessings,
I'll reap.

Arise, Lord;
Again, please save;
To my foes' faces,
Slaps, You once gave,
And the teeth of the wicked
You smashed in past time,
Now bless
With salvation
Your people—
And mine.

Psalm 4

For the Director:
With instrumental music.
A psalm of David.

When I call
Please answer me
And vindicate my right;
When I've suffered
Deep distress
You've relieved my plight;
So, hear my plea
Graciously;
Keep me ever
In Your sight.

O you men
Of little worth
Who slight me
Without pause;
What feeds your lust

After vanity
Or other deviant cause?

Know that God's pious ones
Are His treasured choice;
Whenever I call out to Him
He readily hears my voice.

So, tremble
At your worthless deeds
And do not sin again;
Reflect on them
Before you sleep
And inflict
No more pain.

Duly make your offerings
And trust
In the Lord;
Be witness to doubters
That He grants
Reward.
The joy implanted
Within my heart
As Your special sign
Exceeds that
Of those offering
A harvest of corn and wine;
Enabling me
To slip into sleep
Without a single care
Assured that You
Were offering me
Protection
Beyond compare.

Psalm 5

For the Director.
On nehiloth. A psalm of David.

Lord, hear the anguish
My words contain;
Note my complaint
And my cry of pain.

My king and Lord,
Listen out
For my heartfelt cry;
For with every petition that I make
You readily comply.

You respond to the sound
Of my voice each morn,
And I await Your answer
When I petition You at dawn.

For You are not a God who'll give
Wickedness toleration;
You banish it promptly
From Your habitation.

Scoffers,
From You
Get short-shrift;
You detest evil-doers
And cast them adrift.

Spreaders of lies
You devastate;
Men of violence and guile
You truly hate.

But I enter Your house
Through Your mercy
Most great;
At Your Temple
I bow
And in awe
I wait.

Lord, lead me rightly
Along Your way
Evading ambushers
Who seek to waylay
Me unsuspectingly
To my doomsday.

The direct path
To You,
Reveal;
That a mutual bond
We might seal;
For those enemies' lips
Never utter truth;
They are corrupt within
And wholly uncouth.

Their throat resembles
An open grave;
Their tongue intones
The guile
They crave.

Lord,
Let them suffer
Your condemnation
And fall victim to
Their own machination;
Drive them far

From Your favored nation
For their rejection
Of Your exalted station.

But let all who trust
In You
Rejoice;
Forever raising
A happy voice;
To lovers of Your name
Afford protection;
Let them bask
In Your affection.

Blessings
For the righteous,
Unveil;
Surrounding them
With favor
As with a coat of mail.

Psalm 6

For the Director.
With instrumental music.
On the eight-string harp.
A psalm of David.

Rebuke me not
In Your wrath;
Reprove me not
In Your rage;
Indulge me
In my desperation,
And my pain
Assuage;

Heal me, Lord,
For every bone
Threatens to disengage.

As for my soul—
Even worse
Is its confusion;
How long, Lord,
Will people dub
My faith
An illusion?
So once again
Deliver my soul
From its desperation;
For Your mercy's sake
Save my life
From obliteration.

For once I'm dead
Who'll be there
To sing Your praise?
Can anyone in Sheol
Acclaim Your ways?
I'm so weary
With my sighing;
My abject state
There's no denying.

I lie on a bed
Every night
Drenched
In flowing tears;
My eyes are dimmed
My spirit crushed;
My throat tight
With my fears.

Keep far from me
You evil-doers;
Don't gloat
Or seek my end.
The lord has heard
My lament;
Salvation
He will send.
All my foes
Shall be undone,
Into despair
They'll descend.

Psalm 7

A shiggayon of David,
which he sang to the Lord
concerning Kush, the
Benjaminite.

O Lord, my God,
In whom I trust
Save me from those who pursue;
Lest like a lion
They tear me apart;
None rushing to rescue.

But if ever I
Did the same—
If violence accrued
To my name;
If I harmed those
Who wished me well;
Dragging rivals
Into a bare cell—
Let foes pursue me

In return
And overturn my glory;
Let eternity in the dust
Be the end to my life's story.

Rise, Lord,
With wrath aflame
Against my foes
And their disdain;
The sentence prescribed
By Your law
Invoke on my behalf
Once more.

When a union
Of nations—
On our ruin
Bent—
Surrounds You
Petitioning
Your assent,
Recoil from them
Instantly,
And from their evil intent.

May the Lord who assesses
Every nation
Extend to me
His consideration;
Let my piety secure
My vindication.

The harm of the wicked,
I beg You, frustrate;
Let the worthy enjoy
A happy fate;
The righteous God probes

Man's devotion
And the sincerity
Of his emotion.
I view God
As my shield;
As the upright's savior
He is revealed.

God vindicates
A righteous cause;
Each day
The wicked
To his doom
He draws.

If sharp swords
To scabbards
Are not replaced;
If bows are aimed
At targets in haste;
If weapons of death
Are cruelly prepared;
Arrows randomly shot,
Innocents ensnared—
That arsenal of death
Will incinerate
Those who stock-pile missiles
And shoot them with hate.

Wickedness
They conceive;
Carnage is all
They achieve;
A web of falsehood
They ever weave.

He that lays a trap
Deep in the ground
Will himself fall victim
To the violence around;
To his own head
Will his mischief revert;
Upon his own skull
All his violence and hurt.
So I thank the Lord
For his just ways;
To the Most High
I offer praise.

Psalm 8

For the Director. On the Gittith
A psalm of David.

Lord, God, how majestic
Is Your name on earth;
Let the splendor of heaven
Reflect Your worth.

Already at the babe
And suckling stage
You've implanted in man
The will to engage
Aggressively
With Your foes;
And to vengeance
To become disposed.

When I look at the heavens
Your fingers designed;
The moon and the stars
You have assigned—

How did man figure
In Your grand scheme
And how did he merit
Your esteem?

For You made him
Little less than divine;
Glory and grandeur
In him intertwine;
With dominion over
All Your creation
For benefit
Or exploitation:
Sheep and oxen
Frolicking in the field;
Wild beasts of the forest
Preying concealed;
Birds of the heavens
Fish of the sea
Mammals that glide
On the waves
Care-free
All are the gifts
Of the Lord whose name
On earth has won
Universal acclaim.

Psalm 9

For the Director.
Almuth la-ben.
A Psalm of David

I thank the Lord
With all my heart;
Your numerous wonders
I shall impart.

For You
I reserve
My exultation;
Your illustrious name
Is my jubilation;
When my foes were forced
Into retreat
They stumbled and perished—
A resounding defeat.

For You vindicate
My cause and my right;
From Your seat of justice
Relieving my plight.

Nations
You bitterly denounced;
The wicked
You destroyed;
Their inglorious name
Forever consigned
To the unredeemed
Void.
My foes have all
Been dispatched;
Their homes devastated;
Their cities razed
To the ground—
From memory
Eviscerated.
But eternally
God will remain;
On His throne of justice
He'll forever reign.

With the world
He will deal righteously;

With every nation
Equitably;
The Lord is a refuge
For the oppressed;
In crises,
A haven
For the distressed.

They trust in You
All who know Your Name;
Your followers
You will not disclaim.

To the Lord
Who dwells in Zion
Sing aloud with praise;
Relate to all the peoples
The deeds
That He displays;
For He laments
All innocent blood
When it is violently shed;
The cry of the afflicted
Echoes in His head.

So, Lord,
Grant me mercy
And see my affliction;
Distance me
From those that usher
At the portals of perdition;
That Your deliverance
At Zion's gate
I may recount
And celebrate.

Nations have fallen
Into the pit they made;
Their foot was ensnared
By the trap they laid.

God is renowned
For the justice He seeks;
While the evil man
Is ensnared
By the harm he wreaks.

Let the wicked
Ever be consigned
To Sheol's darkest place;
Those nations who seek to deny
God's ever-saving grace.

For the needy are not
Ignored forever,
Nor are the humble undone
In their modest endeavor.

Arise, Lord, and prevent man
From abusing his power;
Let the nations' acts
Be reviewed
Before You,
Every hour.

Lord,
Strike fear
Into them;
Let the nations admit
That they are
Mere men.

Psalm 10

Lord,
Why do You stand
At such a distance;
Why hide from view
When I need assistance?

When the arrogant wicked
Hound the poor,
Let them fall victim
To the plots they explore.

The power of his lust
Is the wicked man's pride;
Though the bread he breaks
May be sanctified;
Such blessings
The Lord
Will not abide.

The wicked man walks
With haughty gait
Indifferent to
His victims' fate;
He never considers
God's reaction
To the intrigues that give him
Satisfaction.

He appears to prosper
At every turn;
From Your chastisement
He does not learn;
Brushing away his foes
As of no concern.

The wicked say
In their heart,
"From our way of life
We shall not depart;
Adversity
We shall outsmart."

From their mouths
Flow oaths,
Deceit and fraud;
Mischief and evil
They constantly laud.

They lie in wait
In open places;
They slay the innocent
In concealed spaces;
Their eyes alert for
Vulnerable faces.

In a hidden place
They quietly wait;
As a lion in its lair
In a heightened state;
In that way the wicked
Entrap the poor
Spreading the net
To their front door.

They stoop
They crouch
On their knees;
The hapless,
With a leap
They seize;
Saying to themselves,

"God will not recall;
He'll never pursue
Our downfall."

In response, Lord, rise
And strike them down;
Don't forsake the lowly
With their troubled frown;
Why suffer, Lord,
The wicked one's slight
That You don't uphold
The cause of right?

For You do repay
Vice and vexation;
Perpetrators
Of every station;
So that victims may all
Implicitly trust
In the orphan's escape
From the unjust.

Diminish the power of wickedness
And the followers of its way;
Pursue it until you have ensured
It will no longer hold sway.

The Lord reigns
For ever and ever;
From His land,
The wicked
He'll totally sever.

The desire of the humble,
Lord, You hear;
Raising their spirit
And inclining Your ear;

Vindicating the orphan
And the oppressed
That tyrants might cease
Their tyrannical quest.

Psalm 11

I've always trusted
In the Lord;
How dare you say, "Flee
At my word
To the highest mountain
Fast as a bird!"

Just see how the wicked
Bend the bow;
On its string aiming
Their sharp arrow;
Targeting the upright
From the shadow.

When moral foundations
Are thus destroyed
Can righteousness
Really be employed?

Though the Lord is in
His holy place,
His throne gilded
By heaven's grace,
His eyes
Never cease to scan
Nor His gaze to probe
The son of man.

He guides the righteous
Through his trial;

But the wicked and violent
He'll revile.

Blazing coals and Sulphur
On the wicked He'll pour;
A scorching wind shall prolong
The fate they'll endure.

For the righteous Lord
Loves righteous deeds;
To His Presence,
The upright
He directly leads.

Psalm 12

For the Director.
With instrumental music.
On the eight-stringed harp.
A psalm of David.

Help, Lord,
For the pious are no more,
And integrity,
Men choose
To ignore.

When they converse
It is all lies;
Flattering words
They improvise;
Duplicity
They devise.

But God will silence
Flattering lips;
The tongue that

With fabrication
Drips;
That says, "With our words
We shall prevail;
With lips like ours
How can we fail?"

"When the poor
Suffer violence
And the sighs of the needy
Increase,
I shall arise,"
Says the Lord,
"Securing their release."
With that reassurance
He brings them
New-found peace.

The Lord's words
Are perfectly pure
As silver seven-fold refined
In an earthenware crucible—
No dross left behind.

You will preserve
All the deserving
Among this generation
With its ceaseless *yearning.*

The wicked jostle
All around;
When license thrives
They abound.

Psalm 13

For the Director.
A psalm of David

For how long, Lord;
Shall I forever be ignored?
How long till Your Face,
To me
Is restored?

For how long will thoughts
Thrash around in my mind;
How many griefs
Will my heart
Daily
Find;
With triumphs,
To foes alone
Assigned?

Answer me,
O Lord God,
When my plea
You scrutinize;
Enlighten me
Of dangers that
May hasten my demise;
Lest my enemy says,
"I have prevailed";
And foes rejoice
When I have failed.
But When I trust
In Your salvation
My heart shall rejoice;
And I shall sing
A song to the Lord

For His bounties
Most choice.

Psalm 14

For the Director.
For David.

The ignorant man
In his mind
Says "God does not exist";
His degenerate and abhorrent
    deeds,
With goodness,
Make no tryst.

The Lord from heaven
Looks down on man
To discover a perceptive mind;
One that truly seeks Him out
With thoughts
By faith
Refined.

But there are none
To be found;
They're all an abhorrent lot;
Not one of them pursues good—
Not so much as a jot!

How naïve are those evil-doers
Who devour my people like bread!
Because they never acknowledge
    the Lord,
To their doom
They are led.

There they will greatly tremble;
There they will see the light:
God dwelling among the righteous—
A truly wondrous sight.

The counsel of the lowly,
Some of you may discount;
But God is their refuge
And you'll be held to account.

May the deliverance of Israel
From Zion proceed;
When God restores the fortunes
Of His people
With speed;
Then Jacob will demonstrate
A pleasure most intense;
And great joy,
To all mankind
Israel will dispense.

Psalm 15

Lord,
Who may dwell in Your tent;
To your holy mountain
Who'll make the ascent?
The blameless man
Who embraces right;
For whose heart
Truth
Is a delight;
Whose tongue
To slander
Is never host,
But strives to do

His utmost
To avoid wronging
A fellow man,
And was never reproved
By his clan;
Who recoils from those
Of ugly deeds
But honors the pious
And serves their needs;
Whose promise
He would never retract,
Though to his own harm
It might impact;
Whose money
On interest
He has never lent;
Nor accepted a bribe
Against the innocent.

He who lives
A life like this
Will never fail
To attain to bliss.

Psalm 16

A mikhtam-psalm of David

Save me, Lord,
For in You I trust.
I said to God,
"I really must
Acknowledge You
As my guide
For the benefits
You alone provide.

All hail to the holy
Who inhabit our land;
I acclaim you all
As glorious and grand.

But those who rush
To idolatry
Will suffer
Exponentially;
I recoil from the blood
Of their libations;
I avoid their names
In deliberations.

Lord, You are my heritage;
A Toast to you I drink;
My fate is squarely
In Your hands;
My faith,
Our strongest link.

You ensure that I enjoy
A vista of delight;
A legacy of loveliness
My spirit,
To excite.

I bless the Lord
For guiding
My every decision,
When nightly doubts
Tormented me
And clouded my vision.

The Lord's Presence
Has been for me
An ever-present reality;

I shall not slip
For He takes His stand
Protectively
At my right hand.

Therefore, my heart is happy
And my disposition bright;
Every limb of my body
Feels vigorous and light
Knowing You would never
Abandon my soul
Nor consider consigning it
To the depths of Sheol;
Your pious ones
You'd not permit
So much as a glance
Into the pit.

The right path
Wherein life resides
I beg You to disclose;
For in Your holy Presence
Joy overflows,
In abundance
At Your right hand;
Delights forever
You'll command.

Psalm 17

A prayer of David

Lord, hear my cry
For I am sincere;
To my petition
Lend Your ear;
Allow my prayer

To come near;
Let not my lips
To guile,
Adhere.

My justice
You will guarantee;
Your eyes probe
My integrity.

Every night
You choose to test
My inner being
While I'm at rest;
When You explore
What's in my mind
Nothing unworthy
Do You find:
No passing thought
That I expressed
Which, rather,
Should have been
Suppressed.

Man's dealings I measured
By the standards You dictate;
I watched as the lawless
Were doomed to their fate;
I followed the route
Which You had planned
That my feet would not slip
As on shifting sand.

When I call on You
You always reply;
So incline Your ear
To my plaintive cry.

With Your right hand
Bestow on me
Kindnesses to amaze;
You who save the faithful
From all fists
Upraised.

Protect me like the apple
Of Your eye;
Let Your wings conceal me
Till danger passes by;
From the wicked
Who would plunder
All I own;
Foes who would gladly dance
Around *my tombstone.*

Their excesses,
From pity
Make them immune
While their mouths utter
What to them
Is opportune.

Wherever we go
They surround us
On every side;
To survey the entire horizon
Their eyes are open wide.

They are like a lion
Relentless to stalk its prey;
Like cubs lurking
On a concealed path-way.

Arise to confront them
As they prowl around;

Humble them *as they seek*
To bring us all
To ground;
Liberate me
With Your sword
From the wicked
And the base;
Rescue me from tyrants
Undeserving of Your grace;
Free me with Your hand
From worthless men, O Lord,
Those whose base cravings
Obsessively are explored
To ensure their bellies
Are enabled to savor
Every luxury provided
By Your favor;
Enough for their offspring
To be satisfied
And for the next generation
Amply to provide.

But I, through my merit,
Will behold Your face;
When I awake
Euphoric
To enjoy Your grace.

Psalm 18

For the Director. For the servant
of the Lord. For David, who
addressed the words of this song
to the Lord on the day that He
delivered him from the hand of all
his enemies and from the hand of
Saul.

He said,
"Lord I adore You
For making me strong;
You are my craggy fortress
My protection
Life-long."

My God is a mighty rock
My refuge
Secure;
A shield and savior
A tower
That will endure.

The Lord,
Whom I designate
As "ever to be praised";
Out of harm's way,
Ensures
That I am raised.

Death pangs gripped me;
Belial's traps ripped me;
Sheol's cords bound me;
Deadly snares surround me.

To the Lord I called
In my distress;

To my God I cried
With success;
From His Temple
He heard my cry;
My desperate plea
He did not deny.

The earth was seized
With fearful quaking;
Mountains' foundations
Were close to breaking;
Through His displeasure,
Incessant shaking.

Smoke belched out
At His ire;
From His mouth
A devouring fire;
Live coals—
A flaming pyre.

He lowered the heavens
For His descent;
Darkness,
The pathway
To where He went;
He mounted a cherub
Readied for flight;
The wind's wings
Transported Him
To where He would alight.

For His concealment
He summons the dark
Which obscures Him
Like an ark;
The dense clouds

Of the sky
Gift rain as they darkly
Overfly.
At the radiance
Of His glorious Presence
His clouds disperse
And change their essence;
Transformed into icy hail—
Coals of fire
That assail.
To the accompaniment
Of heavenly thunder
The Most High's voice
Tears asunder
The clouds that form into hail—
Coals of fire
That assail.

As missiles
He launches them
Against His foes;
Scattering them
With double blows,
And routing them
With lightning's throes.

The ocean bed
Is exposed to view;
The earth's foundation
Revealed anew
When the Lord's rebuke
Is transmitted
And the breath of His nostrils
Is emitted.

Out of the heights
He grasped my hand;

From the deluge,
Depositing me
On dry land.

He saved me from
A foe most cruel
And from his odious,
Oppressive rule;
When calamity suddenly
Reared its head
He supported me
In my dread;
To a secure terrain
I was steered;
His redemption a sign
That I'm endeared.

Because of my integrity
The Lord will richly reward me;
Because my hands are ever clean
In His love for me
He'll intervene.

For the Lord's ways
I observe;
From His trodden paths
I never swerve.

For all His laws
I keep in mind;
Not one
Do I leave behind.

In that way
His trust I win
That I shall keep myself
Remote from sin.

Because I displayed integrity
The Lord fully rewarded me;
Because my hands were wholly
    clean
As His favored one
I was seen.

With the pious
You deal piously;
With the blameless
Blamelessly;
With the pure
Whole-heartedly;
With the cunning
Cunningly.

The lowly folk
You save from harm;
The haughty-eyed
You disarm.

For You light
The lamp I bear;
Dispelling the darkness
Of my despair.
With Your help
I thoroughly crush
All forces that invade;
I scaled their ramparts
Effortlessly
When to my God
I prayed.

Perfect is
The way of God;
His words are all
Well-honed;

A shield to all
Who make of Him
Their refuge
Enthroned.

For other than God
What deity
Can possibly exist;
And is there another
Reliable rock
That really can assist?

He is the God who girded me
With incomparable might;
He declared the way I trod
As indubitably right.

He made my legs
Like the deer's
Directing me to the height;
Training me
For battles ahead
And keeping me in His sight;
Guiding my arms
To aim an arrow
Of bronze
With which to fight.

You extended to me
Your protective shield;
You held my right hand
In the field;
Your own profile
You kept low;
My success
You placed on show;
Enabling me

To take long strides;
My footstep neither
Slips nor slides.

I pursue my foes
And overtake;
Till they are destroyed
I apply no brake.

Once I've struck
They don't rise again;
At my feet,
They all lie
Slain.

In every battle
I sense Your power,
Constraining my enemies
To cower.

You flip them round
To turn their back;
Readied for my
Deadly attack.

Their cries for help
Are all in vain;
The Lord regards them
With disdain.

Like windswept dust
I grind them down;
Flattened like dirt
On the streets
Of a town.

You make me immune
To the strife of nations;

You appoint me to lead
Their deliberations;
Foreign peoples serve
My aspirations.

When they hear of my exploits
They become compliant;
Like vassal nations
All wholly reliant;

Devoid of courage,
Neutralized;
Exiting from fortresses
Paralyzed.

The Lord lives!
My rock is blessed!
God, as my savior,
Is professed.

The God who grants me vengeance
Treads peoples under my feet;
Redeeming me from enemies,
Making my foes retreat;
From men of violence
Saving me—
My victory
Complete.

That is why
Among the nations
My thanks are uttered loud;
That is why
To praise Your name
I am ever proud.

He will shower salvation
Upon His king;

On His anointed
Success in everything;
To David
And his offspring
Eternal blessing
He will bring.

Psalm 19

For the Director.
A psalm of David.

The heavens declare
The Lord's glory
The skies assert
His handiwork's story;
Each day relates it to the next
Night to night
Its creative text;
No words involved
No description
No sound evoking
Heaven's diction.
Yet to all the world
Its voice reaches
To the earth's far regions
Its message preaches:
That He was the One
Who draped the heavens
Around the sun like a tent;
Confident of the task ahead
And on its mission bent;

Stepping forth as a groom
From his canopy;
As a hero doing a lap of honour
Proud as he can be.

At one of heaven's arcs
It rises,
Heralding a new day;
Forming a blessed circuit
Wending its homeward way;
Universal in its embrace
And the warmth
Of its display.

Perfect
Is the Law of God,
Refreshing the soul;
Offering faithful testimony
To the divine role
In prompting simple folk
For wisdom
To enroll.

Perfect are His precepts
They make the heart rejoice;
Clarity in His commandments
Enlightenment
Through their voice.

Fear of the Lord
Brings a purity
That forever will survive;
Truth nestles in His judgments
That righteousness
May thrive.

More desirable than gold
They are;

Than fine gold in abundance;
Sweeter than honey
Or the honey-comb
Oozing its juicy substance.

Your servant is most zealous
To perform all Your commands,
Knowing a great reward will flow
Directly from Your hands.

For all that,
I am aware
That errors must encroach;
So, clear me of any guilt
When unwitting sins
Approach.

Let the words of
My heartfelt prayer
At all times
Win Your favor;
Lord, my rock
Who redeems from harm,
My piety
May You savor.

Psalm 20

For the Director.
A psalm of David

In the face of all adversity
He will come to your aid;
Jacob's God will remove you far
From any ambush laid.
Help will be dispatched to you
From His holy place;

From Zion's fortress
You'll receive
His ever-saving grace.

The acceptance of all
Your voluntary gifts
He will indicate;
The quantity of your offerings
He'll appreciate.
All the desires of your heart
May He provide;
May no single cherished plan
Ever be denied.

We shall rejoice
At Your salvation;
To our God
Our flag we'll raise;
May He respond
To your every plea,
*And may you ever deserve
His praise.*

Hence my belief that the Lord
Will protect His anointed king;
Responding with power
From His holy heights;
His right hand
Delivering.

There are some
Who trust in chariots
Others in horses' speed;
But we proclaim the name of God
As our eternal need.

The first are destined
To be crushed

And utterly dejected,
While we shall rise
To the heights—
To victory
Directed.

So, save, Lord,
We beg You;
Our king, please respond;
Whenever we petition,
Renew our timeless bond.

Psalm 21

*For the Director
A psalm of David*

Lord
In Your strength
The king rejoices;
In Your salvation
Delight,
He voices.

To all his requests
You acceded;
And did not hold back
When he pleaded.

Goodly blessings
To him You proffered;
A golden crown
For his head
You offered.

When he begged for life
It was extended:
Length of days,

With blessings
Blended.

The victory that You bestowed
His glory,
Enhanced;
Splendor and majesty
To him
You advanced;
For on him You lavish
Unending blessing;
The joy of Your presence
Gladly accessing.
For in the Lord
The king feels secure,
That by His compassion
He will endure.

Your hand destroys
All Your foes;
Your right hand
Raining down salvos.

Like a furnace,
Your wrath
Will set them ablaze;
In Your fiery fury
They are erased;
Their fruit destroyed
From off the earth;
Their seed expelled
As a still-birth
In return for the evil
That they design;
For the dastardly plans
They never refine.

May You turn them around
And put them to flight;
That Your bow may ever
Have them in its sight.
Be exalted, Lord,
For Your strength;
That we may sing our praise
To You at length.

Psalm 22

For the Director.
On Ayyelet ha-Shahar. A psalm of
David.

My God,
My God,
When You forsake me
I truly know not why;
Why You are unmoved
By my plight
And by my plaintive cry;
Why each day
When I call
No answer do I hear;
Why each night
No respite comes
And I am gripped by fear.

But You are Holy
Ever enthroned
On the praise of Israel—
Finely honed.

Our fathers trusted
In You alone;
As reward for that trust

Was deliverance shown.
To You they cried;
They escaped
To a man;
Wholly trusting
In Your higher plan.

But I am no more than a worm—
A man only in name;
I'm scorned by folk
And everywhere
I've become an object of shame.

When they look at me
Clearly, I see
The mockery in their eyes;
I blanch at the insults
Of their lips
That my face they despise.
Nodding at me,
They mock my faith
In ironic mode:
"Let him commit to His Lord
And on Him off-load;
Leaving Him to rescue
With His grace bestowed!"

For You drew me out
Of my mother's womb;
Calming me on her breast;
From birth
I became Your charge—
The start of my spiritual quest.

So, my plea is
Don't stand apart
For trouble is at hand;

And there are none around
To help stave off
The terror
That's been planned.

For I am surrounded by a host
Of bull-like foes;
Mighty bulls of Bashan
In a pack
Enclose;
Their sharp fangs,
At me
They bare;
Roaring lions
Ready to tear.

Like water
I'm poured out on the floor
My bones disjointed
My body sore;
My heart
That strongly used to beat
Now melts like wax
Before the heat.
My strength is brittle
As a shard;
My tongue,
To palate
Sticks so hard;
You've assigned to me
My burial earth;
For a life's toil
Is that my worth?

Like dogs
Attracted to the scent—
A pack of rogues

On evil
Bent—
Surround me
Mauling hands and feet;
Not stopping until
They are replete.

Fleshless
I count my every bone;
The merciless
Watch me
With hearts of stone.

My clothes
Among them
They divide;
For my robes
They cast lots
Far and wide.

So, do not stand
In far-off shade;
My Strong One
Hasten to my aid;
From the slaying sword
Deliver my soul;
From the canine brute
Let me escape
Whole;
From the lion's mouth
Let me be snatched;
From the wild ox's horn
Safely detached.

Then
To my brethren

I'll declare Your fame;
In the congregation
I'll praise Your name.

Praise Him
All you God-fearers;
Honor Him
Jacob's seed;
Be in awe
Israel's offspring
And He'll provide
Your every need.

For God will not scorn
Nor will He spurn
The poor man's
Lowliness;
His Face,
From him,
He'll never hide;
His complaint
He'll assess.

For what You do
I utter praise
Amid the congregation;
Among the pious
I'll pay my vows
At a festive celebration.

The meek will be invited—
Each an honored guest—
They'll eat their fill
And be satisfied;
To the Lord's praise
They'll attest.

"May your hearts be ever
Of good cheer,
Come what may!"
That will be the toast
To the God-fearers
On that memorable day.

Let the far-flung dwellers
On earth consider
And return to the Lord;
Let all the families of nations bow
Obedient to His word.

For kingship is determined
By the Lord's volition;
He rules all the nations *by*
His sovereign
Decision.

All earth's delicacies
The worthy, prostrating, shall eat;
Sharing with the indigent
Who beg in the street;
Whose battle for survival
Ends in defeat.

Their offspring
Shall serve Him
With all their heart;
Affirming to my progeny
The Lord's paramount part.

They shall come and relate
Of His righteousness, sublime;
A heritage for those who'll live
At some future time.

Psalm 23

A Psalm of David

The Lord is my shepherd;
No need does He deny;
In lush pastures
He sets me down;
By tranquil streams
I lie.

The Lord restores
For His name's sake
My spirits
When they are low;
Along right paths
He guides me
Urging me to follow.

Were I to stumble into a gorge
Where death had cast its pall
Your Presence would dispel my fear
And ever I'd walk tall;
Your rod and staff assuring me
I'd never again fall.

You set for me
A table place—
I eat without a qualm—
Surrounded by enemies
Resolved to do me harm.

With oil of the purest kind
My head
You have anointed;
A cup of blessing
Overfull
For me You have appointed.

May grace and kindness
Pursue me all my days
That I may dwell in the Lord's
    house,
Remaining there always.

Psalm 24

For David. A psalm.

To God belongs all the earth
And the bounty it contains;
The world and its inhabitants
Whose fate He ordains.
For, upon the seas
He founded it;
Rivers threading
Its terrains.

Who may ascend
The Lord's mount
With the confidence
That he might count
Among those who are
Chosen to stand
In His holy place
By divine command?

One with clean hands
Whose heart is pure;
Steadfastly disdaining
Shallow allure;
Who has never taken
My name in vain
And entered not
Falsehood's domain.
He shall be blessed

By the Lord
With heaven-sent aid
As his just reward;
Among those of Jacob
Who beseech Your Face,
Holding righteousness
In their embrace.

Raise the height of your lintel
O you Temple gate
For the King of Glory approaches—
The One for whom
We wait.

"What do we know
Of this King of Glory
And His paramount role
In Israel's story?"
"He's the epitome
Of strength and power;
Victorious in battle—
A lofty tower."

So, raise the height of your lintel
O you Temple gate,
For the King of Glory approaches—
The One for Whom
We wait.

"What do we know
Of this King of Glory
And His paramount role
In Israel's story?"
"He's the Lord of Hosts—
What more can one say?—
His royal glory incomparable
In every way!"

Psalm 25

For David.

To You, Lord,
I entrust my soul;
My reliance on You
Shall make me whole;
So my enemies' boasts
Won't take their toll.

Those who look to You
Won't be let down;
It's the faithless
Who shall wear the frown;
Left empty-handed,
with sorrows to drown.

Lord, show me Your paths
And reveal Your ways;
Guide me in truth
And teach me
To praise
You as the God
Of my salvation;
I daily await
Your revelation.

Remember Your mercy
And kindness,
Lord;
From the beginning of time
They have left me
Assured.

Of the sins of my youth
And my transgression,
Do not remind me

Through any expression;
In mercy assess me
As I am now
For the sake of Your goodness
That I avow.

The Lord is good
And wholly upright;
Teaching sinners
To become contrite.

The meek
He guides
In justice's way;
Instructing the humble
To obey.

All the Lord's ways
Are kind and true;
His loyal ones attest
To their value.

For Your name's sake, Lord,
Forgive my sin;
However great,
Let pardon begin.

God-fearers are shown
The path to hand
To achieve happiness
And a life that's grand;
Bequeathing
To their seed
The Promised Land.

The Lord molds His fearers
Into a select clan;

Initiating them into
His covenanted plan.

My eyes are ever to the Lord
In hopeful expectation
That from the trap
He'll release my legs
And end my incarceration.

Turn to me
And be gracious
For alone am I,
Hard-pressed;
My troubles have multiplied—
Relieve me from distress!

With my toil
And my affliction
I beg You
Sympathize;
To pardon
All my many sins
Please speedily arise.

See the vast number
Of my amassed foes;
And the path of fierce hatred
That they all chose.

Watch over me
And save
At this critical hour;
Let me not be undone
For I've trusted
In Your power.

Let my innocence and integrity
Keep me secure;
Because You know
My trust in You
Will ever endure.

So, Lord, redeem Israel
From all its distress
And bestow on her an eternity
Of peace and success.

Psalm 26

For David.

Lord, grant me vindication
For the innocence I display;
In You I always placed my trust
Never wavering
From Your way.

Test me, Lord,
And try me;
Probe my mind and heart;
For Your kindness never leaves
    me—
Truth has led me from the start.

I never sought the company
Of the empty and the vain;
Concealers of their motives
I hold in disdain.
From the company
Of evil men
I recoil in disgust;
With the wicked
I shall never dwell,

Whoever says I must.
I shall wash my hands in innocence;
Your altar
I'll surround;
Eagerly savoring
Thanksgiving's joyful sound;
Acclaiming Your wondrous deeds
To worshippers all around.

Lord
I love Your Temple,
Your holiest abode;
Location of Your glory,
Above all things
Hallowed.
So, let not my soul
With sinners
Be swept away;
Let not my life
Be snuffed out
As violent men
Hold sway.

For while their hands perpetrate
Crafty, treacherous deeds
And their palms are
Outstretched for
Bribery's proceeds,
I walk in innocence
Craving merciful redemption;
My feet resting on firm ground
Through Your intervention
For which I'll ever bless the Lord
Before the congregation.

Psalm 27

A psalm of David

With the Lord as my light
And my salvation
Of whom should I be afraid?
When He is the stronghold
Of my life
Before whom
Should I be dismayed?

When evil men lay into me
To destroy my life—
Enemies and adversaries
Everywhere rife—
It is they that shall all end up
Stumbling and prostrate;
Gaining no advantage
By their jealousy and hate.

So even when surrounded
By a host of hostile foes
I worry not *that they might*
Be added to my woes;
And even should war
Loom large ahead
Even then I shall remain
Wholly devoid of dread!

One request
I make of God—
That alone I seek:
To live out my life
In His sacred house
With the pious
And the meek;

Gazing on the beauty
Of His majesty;
Each Temple visit deepening
The sense of intimacy.

For, when He hides me
In His booth
I'm well out of
Harm's way;
In the secret fastness
Of His tent;
Raised high above
The fray.

Then I'll enjoy victory
Over foes all around;
With festive offerings
In His tent
Amid song and joyful sound.

Lord, hear me
When I cry
And graciously respond;
When I am prompted
To seek Your face
Let us renew our bond.

You who've been
Your servant's help
Hide not Your face from me;
Do not abandon or forsake—
A Savior ever be.

Though father and mother
Neglect me
The Lord will take me in;

Lead me along Your straightest
   path
So my enemies won't win.

Do not subject me
To the whims of my foes;
To false and violent witnesses
With all their lies and blows.

Did I not indeed believe
That one day I'd be blessed
To enjoy the Lord's bounty
And a life of rest?

Put your faith
In the Lord Above;
Let your heart be brave
And strong;
Look to Him
To grant you days,
Happy, good and long.

Psalm 28

For David.

Lord, when I call to You
My rock
Ignore me not;
For if You keep silent
I'm doomed
To the burial plot.

Listen out for the sound
Of my supplication;
Hear me when I cry
In utter desperation;

To Your holy abode
I lift my hands,
To the One alone
Who truly understands.

Don't rank me
With wicked men
Whose goals are full of guile;
Speaking warmly to
Their so-called friends
While duping them
All awhile.

Let them pay the price
That they deserve
For the cause of evil
That they serve;
Let them suffer the pain
That they inflict
When You issue
Your verdict.

For the Lord's deeds
They don't take to heart;
From the work of His hands
They stand apart;
So let them suffer
Devastation;
Deny them
Rehabilitation.

Blessed be
The Lord who hears
My every petition;
The strength and shield
In whom I trust
Made me His acquisition.

My heart rejoices
When through song
I express appreciation;
The Lord will strengthen
Man's resolve
Bestowing approbation
On His anointed
As a tower of strength
And dispenser
Of salvation.

Save Your people
From their foes
And Your heritage
Please bless;
Forever tend and raise them up,
Sustaining their success.

Psalm 29

A psalm of David,

O heavenly beings,
Assign to the Lord
Glory and might;
Acclaim the grandeur of His name
Within the highest height;
Worship Him for the majesty
Of His holiness;
Your songs of praise and thanksgiving
To His great name
Address.

Upon the great waters
God's voice reverberates;
When His glory thunders
Its sound resonates

Over the mighty floods
With a power
That terrifies;
But whose majesty
Encompasses
The earth and the skies.

God's voice splits the cedars—
The cedars of Lebanon—
With a power evocative
Of when the universe began;
Making them skip like a calf
On its unsteady feet;
Lebanon and Syria
Totter and bleat.

The Lord's voice releases
Flames of fire;
The deserts quake
At the sound of His ire;
The Kadesh desert trembles
Before a fate most dire.

At God's command
The hinds calve
And forests
Are stripped bare;
But in His Temple
All acclaim
The glory residing there.

He is the One
Who sat enthroned
At the flood and inundation;
Forever exalted He shall be
In His royal station;
Conveying strength

And lasting peace
To Israel
His cherished nation.

Psalm 30

A psalm of David. A song
For the dedication of the Temple

I exalt You, Lord,
For rescuing me;
For not suffering my foes
To rejoice with glee.
I petitioned You
With my appeal;
Confident You
Would speedily
Heal.

You raised me, Lord,
From Sheol;
Safe from the abyss
You kept me whole.

Sing to the Lord
O pious ones;
To His holy name
Sing praise;
For though His anger
Is momentary
His grace
For a lifetime
Stays.

In the evening
One may lie down
In a flood of tears;

But rise at dawn
Full of joy
No longer plagued by
Fears.

I used to think
With blithe pride
You'd ever be
By my side;
That by Your favor
You'd make me strong
As a lofty mountain—
Confident
Lifelong.

But when You chose
To hide Your face
I sensed the greatest
Fall from grace.
Then to You
I made appeal
Petitioning relief
From my ordeal:
"What is to be gained
By my death;
If I view the pit
With my dying breath?
Can the dust
Utter praise
That You desire?
Can it declare the trust
That You inspire?"

You turned my lament
Into dancing;
Replaced my sackcloth
With joy;

That endless hymns
To You
And praise
I might ever employ.

Psalm 31

For the Director.
A psalm of David

In You, Lord,
I put my trust;
May I never be
Let down;
Let Your compassion
Redeem me
And remove
My permanent frown.

Incline to me
Your listening ear
And deliver me
With haste;
Be for me
As a tower of strength;
A fortress
Strategically placed.

For You are my rock
And citadel;
For Your name's sake
Lead me
To where I should dwell;
Free me from the trap
That has been laid;
You are my stronghold
That none can invade.

To You
My spirit
I commend;
God of truth,
Redemption
Send;
Pursuers of vanities
I detest;
My trust is in God
And to Him
I attest.

In Your lovingkindness
I greatly rejoice;
You saw my trouble,
Heard the strain
In my voice.

You didn't hand me over
Into an enemy's hand;
You set my feet firmly
On broad and secure land.

Have mercy, Lord,
For I am truly
Under duress;
My eyes and inner being
Are wasted with stress.

For I sense my life
Ebbing away
Through the grief
I have endured;
Through years wasted
Bemoaning a fate
That I knew
Could not be cured.

For it was the result of my sin
That my strength gave way
And my limbs just crumbled
Like poorly-baked clay.

I became the butt
Of all my foes;
To my neighbors
A source of mirth;
My friends feared
To take my side;
On-lookers gave me
Wide berth.

Like the dead I vanished
From their mind;
Like a long-lost object
Of a worthless kind.

I heard their widespread
        whispering—
A terror campaign—
Plotting how best to ensure
That I was among the slain.
But in You, Lord,
I put my trust;
"You are my God!"
I said;
My fate is Yours
To save me from
Pursuers
Who want me dead.

On Your servant
Benignly smile;
With kindness
Save me
From men of guile.

When I cry out
Don't disappoint;
Let the bones of the wicked
Be out of joint;
Silenced,
Into Sheol they slip;
On life
They finally
Lose their grip.

Let lying lips
Be struck dumb,
Whose sentiments
Are loathsome;
Denouncing the righteous
In arrogance
With a haughty
Contemptuous
Dissonance.
How great is the good
You've laid in store
For those who display
An abundance of awe;
In the presence of men
It shall be bestowed
On those who take refuge
In Your abode.

Protect them
In Your hidden place
From man's machination;
Shelter them in Your abode
From malicious condemnation.

I bless the Lord
For the wondrous deeds
Of kindness shown to me;

When I fled to him
As those who flee
To a refuge city.

Rashly, I once believed
That by You
I'd been displaced;
But You heard the sound
Of my appeal
And responded
With haste.

Love the Lord
You pious ones;
The loyal
He will guard;
But His revenge
On the arrogant
Will be unduly hard.

Remain strong in your faith;
In your courage
Be steadfast;
That the reward for your loyalty
May be truly vast.

Psalm 32

For David.
A Maskil-psalm

Happy is the man
Whose transgression is pardoned;
Whose sin is erased
For his heart
Was not hardened.

Happy the man
Whose iniquity
The Lord regards
With impunity;
In whose spirit
There is no deceit;
Whose heart is pure
Without conceit.

While I watch in silence
My limbs disintegrate
Weakened by my incessant cries
Lamenting my fate.

By night and by day
Your blows knock me out;
I was languorous
As in a summer's drought.

Then I acknowledged
The gravity of my sin;
I didn't conceal
My guilt within.

"I must confess," I said,
"To God my transgression";
And You absolved me immediately
You heard my confession.

So, let every man of faith pray
When he senses You may be found
That though the floods may
        inundate
He might be safe and sound.

You are to me
As a shelter
Preserving me from distress;

Ensuring that
Victory songs
I constantly access.

So, *friends,* let me instruct you
In the way you should go;
Under my watchful eye
Blessings to you will flow.

Do not behave like a horse
Or as a mule untrained,
That only a bit and bridle
Can render restrained,
That no injury
To you may be sustained.

The wicked may suffer torment;
But he that trusts in the Lord
Will be surrounded by kindness
As his well-deserved reward.

Rejoice in God
You righteous ones
And be overjoyed;
Let the upright all shout aloud
With a gladness
Unalloyed.

Psalm 33

You righteous ones,
With voices raised
To the Lord
Sing aloud;
The upright proffer praises
With perfect faith
Avowed.

With the lyre give thanks
To the Lord
And raise your voice on high;
Let the ten-stringed harp
Enhance your praise
And His glory
Magnify.

Sing to Him
A new song
With music
Skillfully played;
Let the trumpet sound
Loudly proclaim
The faith
To be relayed.

For God's promise
Is trustworthy;
Faithfully
He carries it out;
He loves the charity and justice
Dispensed by the devout;
For the earth is filled with a
    kindness
That assuredly shall sprout.

By the Lord's word
The heavens were made;
By His breath
The planetary schemes;
The ocean's waters
He piled as mounds;
The depths
A basin
For streams.

Let all the earth
Fear the Lord;
Let mankind stand in awe;
For when He spoke
Everything appeared;
By His order
Made secure.

The nations' plans
The Lord frustrates;
Their designs
Are nullified;
His purpose
And His heart's desire
Forever will abide.

Happy the nation
Whose God
Is the Lord alone;
Happy the people
That He chose
To be His very own.

From the heaven
The Lord looks down
And watches the children of man;
From His abode
He monitors
Their every act
And plan.

He it is
Who fashions
Every human heart;
He it is
Who evaluates
Each project that they start.

A large force
Cannot be sure
To protect a head of state;
A warrior's strength
Offers no guarantee
Of his secure fate.
A horse provides
Vain hope
Of victory secured;
In the great power of its limbs
Escape is not assured.

The eye of the Lord
Oversees
His God-fearing folk;
Those who await His mercy
And lovingly
Bear His yoke;
To deliver them
From certain death
And from famine
The beasts of their field;
We place our hope in the Lord
Who is our help and shield.

In Him
Our hearts fully rejoice;
In His holy name
We trust;
Reward, Lord,
Our faith in You;
Your care
Extend to us.

Psalm 34

For David. When he feigned madness before Abimelech, who drove him out, and he left.

I bless the Lord
At all times
With the praise of my mouth
Unending;
The humble rejoice
When they hear
My fervent praise
Ascending.

Declare the greatness
Of the Lord;
Let your voices join with mine;
Together we'll acclaim
The hallowed name
Of the One who is divine.

When I sought the Lord
His answer came
Without a moment's delay;
All the terrors
Surrounding me
He kept well at bay.

His petitioners
All acquire
A radiance unique;
No downcast or worried look
Will ever mar
Their cheek.

An afflicted man
When he cries out

Wins the Lord's attention;
In all his troubles
He receives
Divine intervention.

A Lord's angel
Is stationed
Around all who display awe
To offer a protection
That He'll never withdraw.

Savor how good the Lord is;
Savor it and see.
Happy the man
Whose refuge
He shall always be.
Fear the Lord
All of you
With holiness in view;
They that fear Him
Shall lack for naught;
But shall all
Receive their due.

Lions may endure
Extreme starvation;
Those that seek the Lord
Suffer no deprivation.

Come my sons
Hear what I say;
To the fear of the Lord
I'll point the way.

Show me the man
Whose life's desire

Is to greater goodness
To aspire.

Withhold your tongue
From speaking ill;
Your lips
From uttering guile.
Reject evil,
And good pursue;
To peace
Be ever servile.

Toward the righteous
Is the Lord's gaze;
His ears
Hear their cry;
Against evil-doers
His face is set;
Their memory
He'll deny.

When the righteous cry
The Lord hears;
From their trouble
They are redeemed;
To the broken-hearted
The Lord is close;
To the crushed
Redemption
Is beamed.
Though a righteous man
May be beset
By troubles galore;
From all of them
The Lord will act
As dependable savior.

All his bones
He'll keep intact;
Not one of them shall break;
But the wicked
Are doomed
By the evil they do—
And they make a costly mistake.

For those that hate
Righteous men
Shall wholly be undone;
But His trusty servants
He'll redeem;
They'll know
No vexation.

Psalm 35

For David

Lord, I beg You
Plead my cause;
Fight those
Who now fight me;
With shield and buckler
Arm Yourself;
Rise up,
My helper
Be!

With spear and javelin
Direct Your aim
At foes
Who now pursue;
Take up the cry
On my behalf:

"Your salvation
I value."

Let all who seek
To end my life
Be frustrated
And put to shame;
Let all who plan
To do me harm
Suffer eternal blame.

As the wind-blown chaff
Let them become;
The Lord's angel
Contriving
That they succumb.

Dark and slippery
Be their way;
The Lord's angel
Leading them
To disarray.

For without cause
A trap they set
So that I might fall;
For no reason
A pit they dug
That headlong
I might sprawl.

Unannounced,
May disaster
Overtake them all;
May the net they hid
To target me
Catch them

In its trawl;
In the calamity
That they create
May they be the first
To fall.

Then shall my joy
In the Lord
Be great;
At His redemption
Glee galore;
All my bones shall say,
"Lord, who is like You,
So swift to save the poor
And needy from those
Who exceed them in strength
And, by theft,
Their wealth procure?"

Malicious witnesses appear,
Demanding my corroboration;
Of matters I know nothing of,
They expect my affirmation.
They repay me evil
For any good
I might render
To their cause;
Bereavement of spirit
They create
And confusion
That at me
Gnaws.

Yet, when they were ill
Sackcloth I donned;
With fasting
I afflicted my soul;

Would that their good
For which I prayed
Might redound
To make me whole!

Like one lamenting
A friend or brother,
Distracted,
I went around;
Like one mourning
His own mother,
To gloom
I was bound.

But when I stumbled
In my tracks
There assembled to gloat
A motley mob of strangers,
Aiming non-stop
At my throat;
With a grotesquely mocking
Impious inflection
They gnash their teeth
In my direction.

For how long
Will You stand back
Before rescuing me
From their attack;
And the life
Through which I blissfully glide
From collision with
A lion's pride?

Give me
Ample cause for thanks
Amid a great

Congregation;
Give me leave
To praise You
Among
A mighty nation.

Let lying enemies
Never rejoice
At my undoing;
Or those that hate me
Without cause
And wink
At the hurt ensuing.

For they do not speak
From friendship;
But against those
Who seek no harm
Deceitful schemes they devise
With disarming charm.

They open their mouths
Volubly;
Baying, "Aha! aha!
How great to see
His misery!"—
They bellow
From afar.

Lord, You have seen it all;
Your silence
Do not keep;
Do not stay distant;
To my side
Speedily leap.

Wake up!
Rise
To plead my cause!
My Lord, my Lord,
Come wage my wars.

Judge me
In Your righteousness,
O Lord, my God;
Let them not gloat
Over me
Nor wield
Their threatening rod;
Let them not say
To themselves,
"Aha! we've had our way!"
Let them not claim,
"We've swallowed him up!
We've surely made him pay!"

Let shame and confusion
Befall those happy at my harm;
May those who lord it over me
Meet dishonor and alarm.

But let all who seek
My vindication
Sing with joyful pride:
"Let the Lord
Who desires his servant's peace
Be greatly magnified."

Then my tongue
Will never cease
The whole day through
To declare Your righteousness
And my praise of You.

Psalm 36

For the Director.
For the servant of God.
For David

I know
Beyond a shadow of doubt
The evil the wicked man
Talks about;
Fear of God
Will never arise
As an option
Before his eyes.

For he is entrapped
By the seductive glance
Offered by his sin;
He hates it
When men expose
The evil he harbors within.

Malicious and deceitful words
His lips articulate;
No noble thought can gain access
To change his mental state.

Mischief he plots
As he lies
On his bed each night;
One walking such a crooked path
Rejects no evil
In sight.

Your kindness, Lord,
Reaches up
To the heavens above;
Your faithfulness

To the skies
Is impelled
By love.

Your righteousness is awesome
Like the highest mountain peak;
Your justice
Penetrates the depths
To vindicate the weak;
To Your distressed creatures—
Whether man or beast—
Your saving grace You extend
From the greatest to the least.

How precious is the kindness
Dispensed by Your hand;
For those in the shadow of Your
   wings
There's refuge on demand.

The rich delicacies
Of Your house
They enjoy to their hearts' desire;
You let them drink
From Your refreshing stream
As much as they require.

For with You is
The fountain of life
To sustain all mankind;
In Your light
We see the light—
Enlightenment of the mind.

Dispense Your abundant kindness
To Your devotees;
Let the upright deserve their role
As Your beneficiaries.

Let not the boot of the arrogant
Kick me when I'm down;
Let not the hand of the wicked
Drive me out of town.
There lie the evil-doers—
All cut down to size;
Defeated forever
And powerless to rise.

Psalm 37
For David

At the antics of evil-doers
Do not fret;
At the actions of wrong-doers
Don't get upset.

For they shall wither
Like the grass;
As the green herb
They shall fade;
So put your trust
In the Lord;
Do good
And be repaid:
Enabled to live in your land
With faith fully displayed.

Then you shall glory in the Lord
And He'll grant your heart's desire;
Commit your way to Him with
    trust
And He'll provide all you require.

As the brightness of the morning
    light
Your righteousness He'll display;

And the justice of your cause assert
Like sunshine at midday.
Be patient and wait for God
With sincere expectation;
Make no attempt to express
Naive protestation
When the schemes of rogues
Appear to win
General approbation.

Desist from wrath;
Fury forsake;
Anger will only
Fuel heartache.

For the wicked
Will be banished
Out of hand;
But those who wait for the Lord
Will inherit the land.

In a short while
The wicked
Will vanish from the scene;
You will search in vain and find no
    trace
Of where they had been.

Only the lowly
Shall inherit the land;
With tranquility of peace
Everywhere at hand.

The rogue,
Against a righteous man
Devises schemes;
Gnashing at him with his teeth

Eliciting screams.
The Lord laughs aloud at him
With utter derision
For his doom looms large within
The Almighty's clearest vision.

Swords are drawn by the wicked
And their bows are speedily bent
To fell the poor and needy
Slaying those of pure intent;
Yet those very swords shall pierce
Their wielders' own heart;
And the sturdiest of their bows
Shall be broken apart.

More satisfying to the righteous
Is the little they possess
Than the great abundance
That the wicked process.

The arms of the wicked
Are broken in pieces;
But the Lord supports the
    righteous,
And their bonds
Releases.

As for the blameless
In their deeds:
The Lord surveys
All their needs;
An everlasting portion,
To them all
He feeds.

In adversity
They shall never come to grief;

In famine
They will eat their fill
And always find relief.

For the wicked shall perish—
As befits the Lord's foes—
Like furnace fuel they'll vanish
Leaving smoke
That billows.

A wicked borrower
Does not repay;
But a righteous one
Generously
Gives away.

Those blessed by Him
Will inherit the land;
Those He curses
Will be banned.

If a man steps into prosperity,
From the Lord
It proceeds;
A clear indication that
With him
He is pleased.

But if he also seems to fall
It's not a permanent state,
For the Lord will support his hand
And restore his happy fate.

From when I was a young man
Till now in my old age
I have never encountered
Such an outrage
As a righteous man abandoned

Without support, unfed;
With his offspring
Left to begging
For its daily bread.

The righteous man
Will willingly lend
To those who are in need;
What a blessed heritage
To leave to one's seed!
Flee from evil-doing
And pursue what is right;
Then you will bask forever
In eternity's light.

Because the Lord loves justice
His faithful He won't neglect;
While they'll be safe forever
He'll assuredly reject
The offspring of the wicked
With whom He won't connect.

The righteous
Will inherit the land
That is theirs for eternity;
Wise are the words
Of righteous men
That convey probity.

The law of his God
Is in his heart;
His feet will never slip;
While the wicked stalk
The righteous man
To place him
In death's grip.

But God will not surrender him
Into the wicked one's hand;
And on the day of judgment
Won't condemn him out of hand.

So, wait for the Lord
And keep to His way
That He may exalt you
And forever you might stay
In the land of your inheritance
With your enemies
At bay;
And you shall be a spectator
Of wicked men's
Doomsday.

I have seen a rogue
Wielding power
Like a native plant
Well-rooted;
Yet when I sought him
Gone he was—
Some wiser man recruited!

Mark him that leads
A blameless life
And does all that is right;
For the man of peace
Earns for himself
A future that is bright.

As for transgressors
They'll be destroyed;
The wicked one's future
Rendered
Null and void.

Salvation for the righteous comes
From the Lord on high;
A strong-hold
In troubled times
To calm their tearful sigh.

The Lord is their helper;
Their rescuer
In good time;
Their haven
From the wicked
For displaying trust
Sublime.

Psalm 38

A psalm of David.
For remembrance.

Reprove me not, Lord,
In Your wrath;
Lead me not in anger
On chastisement's path.

For I feel Your arrows
Penetrate;
The blows of Your hand
As a dead weight.

For in my body
Not a limb is sound
Because of Your fury
All around.

None of my bones
Are intact;
For sin

Against me
Is heavily stacked;
My iniquity piles
Over my head;
Weighing me down,
Heavy as lead.

My wounds fester
And they smell
Because of the folly
In which I excel.

I'm bent and cowed
Face to the ground;
All day in gloom
I wander around.

A burning sensation
Grips my loins;
No healing
To my flesh
Adjoins.

Numb I am
And crushed to the core;
A mind in turmoil
I roar and roar.

Lord, all my desires
To You
Are known;
You do not miss
My slightest groan.
I palpitate;
My strength fails;
The luster in my eye
Pales.

Friends and colleagues
Keep their distance
From a plague
To which there's no
Resistance;
Even my relatives
Stand aloof
With a look
Of stern reproof.

Those who seek my life
Lay their snares;
Lies and malice
Are my detractors' wares;
Their deceit more fluent
Than their prayers.

But I act deaf
Choosing not to hear;
Appearing dumb,
Betraying
No fear.

It comes as second nature
Pretending not to hear;
Allowing oneself no retort;
Not so much as a sneer!

For You
Patiently I wait;
Lord, God, attend
To my sorry state.

For I knew they'd gloat
When my foot slipped;
That they'd lord it over me
When I tripped.

For I was near
To collapse;
My pain was prone
To relapse.

When my iniquity
I declare
My sin becomes
My worst night-mare.

For my enemies are strong
And full of life;
My foes abundant;
Their lies rife.

They repay me evil
In place of good;
When I seek their welfare
They return
Falsehood.

So, Lord,
Do not forsake me
Nor stand so far away;
Hasten to help me;
Put Your salvation
On display.

Psalm 39

For the Director. For
Yeduthun.

A psalm of David

I was full of good intentions
To evade sin's invitations;
To place a curb on my lips
In response to the wicked
And their quips.

No response did I make,
I was wholly silent;
No good
Could I look forward to,
My pain was truly violent;
Fever building up inside,
Each thought
A fire
Spreading wide;
Until my tongue
Just had to speak:
"Tell me, Lord,
Why I'm so weak;
Why my life-span
Is so short;
Why into the abyss
I deserved to be brought;
Why, like hand-breadths,
My days
You've measured;
Before Your eternity
Can they be treasured?
As a mere breath

Is man's duration;
A nothingness
Is his proud station.

"As a specter
Man glides around;
Vanity
In his every sound;
Amassing wealth at every turn—
For his heirs to squander
Or to spurn.

"So now, Lord,
In whom shall I trust
If not in You
As I know
I must?

"From all transgression
Deliver me;
The butt of the base
Don't let me be;
For then,
Dumb
I'd have to remain
As before a decree
From Your domain.

"From Your plague
I beg release;
At the blow of Your hand
My life must cease;
Rightly You chastise
A man for sin;
Gnawing at His glory
Like a moth within;

For he is no more
Than a breath
Taken in.

"So hear, Lord,
My earnest prayer;
Respond to my cry
Of despair;
From my tears do not
Stand aloof;
We've become estranged—
What a tragic truth!
A transient dweller
Like my fathers before;
Nothing is permanent;
Nothing's for sure.

So, look away
And let me recover
Before I leave this life
For the other!"

Psalm 40

For the Director.
For David, a psalm.

Patiently I waited for God
And He inclined His ear;
He listened out
For my cry
And heard it loud and clear.

He raised me
Out of a miry pit
With soggy clods of clay;

He set my feet on solid rock;
For my footsteps
A mainstay.

He put in my mouth
A new song;
A hymn for the God
For whom we long;
Encountering this
Many were overawed;
Their flagging faith
Fully restored.
Happy the man
Who has made Him
The object of his trust;
Who keeps aloof
From the arrogant
Who, after lies,
Lust.

Lord, my God,
You have performed
Many a glorious deed;
With wondrous plans
For us
Devised—
All others
You exceed;
When I try
To relate them all
They're too many
And varied.

Neither sacrifice nor meal-offering
You requested me to bring;
Obedience You held aloft

As the most important thing;
Burnt or sin-offerings
For You had no meaning.

This prompted me to declare,
"Here now I have come;
With the scroll of Your law
To demonstrate
That Your will
I've always done."
Indeed, my God,
That is all
I've ever desired:
That with Your law
My inner being
Would be
Wholly fired.

Your righteousness
I relayed
To a great congregation;
You know I never
Restrained my lips
From expressing
Your adoration

Your righteousness
Within my heart
I never concealed;
Your steadfast deliverance
I readily revealed;
From the great congregation
I never hid
All the many kindnesses
You graciously did.
The compassion

You direct at me
You will never withhold;
It is by Your steadfast love
That I am consoled.

For the troubles that surround me
Are too numerous to count;
My iniquities catch up with me—
Truly a vast amount:
More than I could envisage
Or than the hairs of my head;
My heart totally fails me
And I am filled with dread.

Ever may it be Your desire
To save my life;
Hasten to help me
And to remove my strife.

May those that target me
To sweep my life away
Be ashamed and frustrated
Without delay;
May all who seek my harm
Be stopped in their tracks;
May they be confounded
In all their attacks.

Let desolation come upon
Those who act shamelessly
Jeering, "Aha!" and "Aha!" —
Levelling insults at me.

May all those that seek You
Be happy and rejoice;
Affirming Your salvation

They shall raise a vigorous voice,
Saying, "The Lord is great forever;
He's our eternal choice."

Though I am poor and needy
I am the Lord's concern;
My help and my deliverer—
Delay not
Your return.

Psalm 41
For the Director.
A psalm of David

Happy is he
Who shows concern
For those who suffer
A down-turn;
When he endures
Severe privation
The Lord will show him
His salvation.

The Lord will guard
And preserve him alive;
In all his pursuits
Urging him
To thrive;
So surrender him not
To foes
Who connive.

The Lord will sustain him
On his sick-bed;
Not a single ailment
He'll permit to spread.

When I uttered the plea:
"Lord, be gracious to me;
Heal my body
Though I've sinned grossly,"
My foes responded
With words that deride:
"When will he die
With his name
Nullified?"

If one sits by my bedside
He aimlessly speaks;
The ill-will he harbors,
Once outside
He leaks.

All my foes' whisperings
Ever expand;
A torrent of evil
Against me
They've planned:
"May an incurable ill
Attach to him;
From where he lies
May he raise no limb."

Even the friend
That I trusted—
Who shared my food—
For my downfall
Lusted;
But I beg You, Lord,
Show me Your grace;
Raise me up
To put them
In their place.
Then I'll know

That I have Your favor;
When no foe will gloat
Or victory
Savor.

You will support me
And my virtue
You'll affirm;
That in Your Presence
I might stand
Long-term.

Blessed is the Lord
God of Israel;
For all eternity
He shall prevail;

With "Amen, Amen,"
His name we shall hail.

Book 2

Psalm 42

For the Director. A Maskil-
psalm.
Of the Korahites.

As a hind at the streams
Desperate to drink
So I yearn for You—
Of nothing else
I think.

I thirst
For the living God
To be near;
Before His Presence
When might I appear?
My tears were my food
By day and night
As they incessantly taunted,
"Is your God out of sight?"

Those sneers
I still often recall
And feel nauseous as one
Who has swallowed gall;
Contrast the memories
Of when I queued
With the Temple crowd
As it viewed
A joyful spectacle
At the house of God;
Thanksgiving on the path
That pilgrims trod.

Why my soul
Are you so depressed?
Why my chest
Do you feel compressed?
Have faith in God
That He'll bring salvation
That you may live to praise Him
In His habitation.

O my God, I'm so depressed
That from far-off places
My prayers are addressed:
From Jordan, Hermon,
And Mount Mizar—
All from the Holy Land
So far.

Deep to deep
Joins its call;
A roar—
The sound of a waterfall;
All the breakers
And waves You send,
Upon me
They violently descend.

By day
May God bestow on me
All His faithful care,
So that by night
In song my love
Of Him I might declare;
To the One who sustains my life
I offer my fervent prayer.

To God, my rock,
I complain:
"Why do You neglect
My needs;

Why must I walk
Enveloped in gloom
By the stress
Of my foes' deeds?"

My oppressors threaten
To crush my bones;
"Where is your God?"
They taunt;
Why wonder that I am depressed
Or that my spirit is so compressed
When such lack of faith
They flaunt?

Declare your hope
In God above;
May I yet have cause
For praise;
For I know
His salvation shall be
Displayed in many ways.

Psalm 43

Defend me, Lord
And champion my cause
Against a faithless
Nation;
Deliver me
From crafty men
And their devious
Deliberation.

For if You are my strong-hold
Why cast me aside;
To wander around sullenly,
By foes,
Terrified?

Send me Your light
And Your truth
To serve as my guides;
Directing me
To Your Holy hill
Where Your Presence
Resides.

Then I shall approach
The altar of God
Who is my joy and delight;
And I'll praise You
With the lyrical lyre
As the God
Who is ever in sight.

So why am I so depressed
And my spirit so compressed?
Have faith in God
To bring salvation,
When I shall praise Him
In His habitation.

Psalm 44

For the Director.
For the Sons of Korah.
An Instruction.

With our own ears
We heard it clearly,
From parents
Who described sincerely
The deeds You performed
In their time;
In the early years
Of their prime.

You were the One
Who with hand so strong
Dispossessed nations
For doing wrong;
You planted us there
In their place,
And banished them
In disgrace.

For it was not by the sword
That they conquered that land;
It was not their arm
That won victories grand;
It was Your right hand
And Your Presence so bright;
For on them was focused
All Your delight.

For You God
Are truly my king;
For the sake of Jacob
Victory
You bring.

With Your aid
All our foes
We gore;
In Your name
Enemies
We tread to the floor.

For I put no trust
In my bow,
That from my sword
Victory would flow.

For You have saved us
From our foes;

Escalating
Our enemies' woes.
In God we glory
Throughout each day;
Praise to Your name
We ever convey.

But You have been known
To spurn us
And expose us to disgrace;
At the head of our armies
Refusing to take Your place;
From before our foes
You made us retreat;
So that freely they pillaged
Savoring our defeat.

You allowed them to devour us
Just like sheep;
Dispersed among nations—
Our hopes put to sleep;
You sold Your people
For naught in return;
No profit from selling
Did You discern;
Among our neighbors
You made us a disgrace;
A mockery and laughing-stock
All around the place.

Among nations
You made us
An object
Of scorn;
They were amazed
At how we'd become
Outworn;

I was conscious of my
Relentless disgrace;
Abject shame totally
Covered my face
At those who taunted
And reviled;
At enemies
Whose vengeance
Was violent and wild.

Yet, while all of this befell us
We did not disobey;
Your sacred Covenant
We did not betray;
Our hearts never
Went astray;
Neither did our feet
Depart from Your way.

Yet You crushed us
Within a place
Where even jackals
Feel confined;
Enveloping us
In a darkness
Deep enough
To scare the mind.

Had we forgotten
Our God's name
Or spread our hands
To idols vain,
Would He not have known
That we'd done so,
He that knows
How human intrigues
Grow?

For Your sake
We were incessantly
Slain;
Like sheep dispatched
With cold disdain.
So rouse Yourself;
Wake up! Why sleep?
Don't forever forsake
Your very own sheep.

Why do You
Conceal Your face
Putting us under duress?
Why do You appear to ignore
Our affliction
And our stress?

For our life has descended
As low as the ground;
Our body
To earth
Seems totally bound.

So, arise now
And come to our aid;
Redeem us
That mercy
May be displayed.

Psalm 45

*For the Director. Al Shoshanim.
Of the Korahites. A Maskil-
psalm
A love song.*

My heart quivers
With elation
At the thought of reciting
My literary creation
Before the king
Of our nation;
My tongue speaks
With the skill
Of an expert scribe
Employing his quill.

Among the young men
Of your court,
Your beauty
Is unsurpassed;
The words you articulate
In a setting of grace
Are cast;
Your God-sent blessings
Shall forever
Last.

With your warrior sword
Strapped to your thigh
Your splendor and glory
Delight the eye;
Gloriously ride
To success
In pursuit of truth
To provide redress

For the meek
Who walk
In righteousness.

Your right hand
Points out the way
To more awesome deeds
As you enter the fray;
At your arrows most sharp
People fall at your feet;
The king's enemies' heart
Is pierced
In defeat.

Your throne
By the Lord's grace
Shall forever endure;
And the administration
Of your reign
Shall be just
And pure.

Righteousness
Is what You love;
Wickedness
You abhor;
Hence the Lord
Anointed you
With oil of gladness
More
Than any of your courtiers
Ever dreamt you'd have in store.

Myrrh, aloes and cassia
Make fragrant all your clothes;
From your ivory-clad palaces
Lute music outflows

For your entertainment
And that of your fellows.

Princesses form
Your royal escort;
At your right hand
The king's consort
Decked out in Ophir's finest gold—
What a joy to behold!"

Hear me royal daughter,
See and incline your ear;
Forget your folk
And your father's house,
And be of good cheer.

Let the king feast on your beauty
For he is now your lord;
Prostrate yourself
And show him
How much he is adored.

The daughter of Tyre—
The wealthiest nation—
Will flatter you with diverse gifts
To cement the association.

The royal princess
In all her glory
Is conducted within;
A gown of threaded gold
She dons
Before the nuptials begin.
Under embroidered banners
She is led to the king;
Her companions follow her
As maids-in-waiting;

With joy and gladness,
To the palace
They're all brought;
To enter the service
Of the king's consort.

Your sons' distinction
Within the royal line
Shall exceed that of your
    ancestors—
Albeit noble and fine.
You'll appoint them
As officials
Throughout the land;
Wielding authority
By your command.

When I celebrate you
In my verse
For future generations
Peoples will forever add
Laudatory citations.

Psalm 46

For the Director.
For the Korahites.
Al Alamoth. A song.

God is our refuge
And our strength;
A help in trouble,
Always near;
So, if earth were to suffer
Seismic change
We would never
Give in to fear;

Nor would we
If the mountains
Toppled into the sea;
Its waters erupting
Into a tsunami;
Nor if in its swell
The mountains themselves
Were to collapse
Overwhelmingly.

There is a river,
And its streams
Make God's city rejoice;
Of all the holy sanctuaries
It ranks as His first choice.

God resides in its midst,
It shall never be replaced;
He'll inaugurate there
A new dawn—
A day uniquely graced.

Nations disintegrate—
Kingdoms destroyed in a day;
One thunderous word
Uttered by Him,
And the earth shall melt away.

The Lord of hosts
Is with us;
He is to us as a tower;
As the God of Jacob
He demonstrates
His power.

Come and see
How the Lord devised
Widespread devastation;
A prelude to the abolition of war
Between every nation;
Breaking the bow
Shattering the spear;
Chariots
In conflagration.

So, desist from now
And acknowledge well
That I am indeed
The Lord;
Exalted among the nations
And by all on earth
Most awed.

The Lord of hosts
Is with us;
He is to us as a tower;
As the God of Jacob
He demonstrates
His power.

Psalm 47

For the Director.
For the Sons of Korah.
A psalm.

All you peoples
Clap your hands;
Raise your voice to God
In song;
For awesome is the supreme king

Who rules
The earth's throng.

He subjects peoples
To our desire;
Our feet crush nations
Into the mire.

An inheritance,
He chose to bestow,
As Jacob's pride
To whom His love
Would flow.

God ascends
At the trumpet sound;
With the horn's crescendo
All around.

Sing to God
Sing aloud;
Sing to our king
With joyful sound.

For He is king
Over all the earth;
Sing a *Maskil*-hymn
For all you're worth.

In it declare
That now He reigns
Over all the nations
And their domains;
His holy throne
He occupies;
Strict justice
He applies.

The nobles of the nations
Are all welcomed in
As most loyal followers
Of the God
Of Abraham's kin;
For He marshals
To His cause
The protectors of His world
Who respect the laws
Of the exalted One
Whom Israel adores.

Psalm 48

A song. A psalm of the Korahites.

Great is the Lord
And exceedingly acclaimed;
In the city of our God
His holy mount
Is famed.

Majestic elevation;
The earth's greatest pride;
City of the great king
On Mount Zion's
Northern side.

God is perceived
As a tower
And a soaring citadel;
When confederate kings
Commence their siege
They look and they marvel
Before terror overtakes them
Frustrating their counsel.

Trembling seizes hold of them;
They are rooted to the spot;
Like a woman in labor
Writhing on her cot.

Your east wind
You employed
As a ram
With which to batter
The entire fleet of Tarshish—
And into flotsam
Shatter.

What we heard from ancestors
We saw with our own eyes
In the city of our Lord of hosts—
God's city
National prize—
May He sustain it forever
As the focus of our lives.

In Your Temple
We reflect
On Your kindness
And its effect;
The praise we offer
Like Your name
Extends far and wide,
To the very ends of the earth
Wherever men reside;
Victory
By Your right hand
Generously supplied.

Let Mount Zion be happy
And Judah's towns rejoice
As recipients of Your judgments
And objects of Your choice.

Walk around Zion
And encircle her bounds;
Count her towers;
Admire all her surrounds.

Be impressed by her ramparts;
Her citadels
Climb;
Describe for your descendants
That city most sublime;
For He shall remain our God
Until the end of time;
His role as our leader
He shall regard as prime.

Psalm 49

For the Director. For the
Korahites.
A psalm.

Hear this all you peoples,
Listen attentively;
All inhabitants of the world
Listen well to me.

Whether you are of low estate
Or of privileged birth;
Whether you are rich or poor
My words are of great worth.

For my mouth offers wisdom
And my mind profound insight;
I've distilled proverbs and riddles
Bringing their thoughts to light;
Against the background of the harp
My theories I present;
And to the issues of your life
You'll find them congruent.

So, in time of trouble
Why should I be afraid;
When surrounded by deceivers
With hostility displayed?

They who trust in riches
And in how much they possess
Will find none to bail them out
Or grant them access;
Not even a brother
Can offer to pay
The ransom demanded
By God on that day.

The price of a man's life
Is far too high;
To his eternity he must
Say goodbye!
No living forever—
Just the grave
Close by!

For all can see
That wise men die;
Like the fool and the vile,
None can defy
What is their ordained fate:
Leaving to others
Their cherished estate.

Their eternal home
Is but the grave—
Generations' dwelling-place;
Even the earth's most famous
Vanish without trace;
Man's glory is so fleeting,
As the beast's life it's soon gone
He leaves behind the trophies
That all his efforts won.

Naïve is man's confidence
That his words may still be quoted
When he has shed his mortal coil
By those who'll remain devoted.

To Sheol
They shall be directed;
Death shepherding them along;
At salvation's dawn,
To the upright
Their wealth shall all belong.

While in Sheol
Their form decays—
An end to the splendor
Of their displays!
But God shields me
From Sheol's greed,
Summoning me to Him
With the utmost speed.

So, do not fear
When a man grows rich
And his substance multiplies;
Nothing of it will he take at death—
It won't join him where he lies.

Though in his lifetime he may
   boast—
Praise always follows success!—
He will soon join his ancestors
Who to light have no access.

When too much wealth comes
   one's way
Good sense often does not stay;
And man becomes no more than
   beast—
At death
No legacy released.

Psalm 50

A psalm of Asaph

The Lord God spoke;
The world was addressed;
From the sun's eastern rise
To its setting
In the west;
From Zion's matchless beauty
Was His Presence manifest.

God appears;
He won't hold His peace;
His herald a consuming fire–
With destruction released;
Surrounding Him
A tempest—
Turmoil increased.

Heaven and earth
He musters
For the judgment of His folk:
"Welcome, my devotees

You whom I convoke
To seal with Me a Covenant,
Amid sacrificial smoke."

The heavens reiterate
The righteousness of the Lord;
That, His divine justice
To equity is moored.

"Hear, my people Israel
For I shall have my say;
As the Lord your God
My testimony
I shall now convey:

"My reproof is not for neglect
Of any sacrifice;
Your continuous offerings
More than suffice;
I do not claim any bull
From among your herd;
Not a single he-goat
That you had sheltered.

"For every scrubland animal
Belongs to Me;
Across a thousand ranges,
Far as the eye can see.
I know the location
Of the birds on every hill;
Every insect in the fields
Enjoys my good-will.
If I suffered hunger
I would not come to you;
For Mine is the entire world,
With everything on view.

"Do I need to eat bull's flesh
Or drink the blood of a goat?
Gratitude offer to Me;
Charitable vows
Promote.
Then call on Me in trouble—
You will have earned the right—
And honour Me
For rescuing you
From your desperate plight."

God then addressed the wicked:
"Who are you to recite
My laws and the terms
Of my covenant—
Pretending insight—
When in fact you hate discipline
And put My words to flight?

If ever you come across a thief
You make him an associate;
The company of adulterers
You choose to venerate;
Your mouth utters language
That is degenerate
And your tongue and guile choose
To affiliate.
In company you would
Malign your brother
And readily defame
The son of your mother.

"If I kept silent when you did this
You'd think we were the same;
Hence my condemnation
And apportionment of blame.
Pay heed to this all of you

Who ignore the Divine,
Lest I tear you apart with none
To offer a lifeline.

"In your sacrifice of thanksgiving
My honor is on display;
But my salvation is only on offer to
    him
Who changes his way."

Psalm 51

For the Director.
A psalm of David,
when Nathan the
prophet came to him
after he had consorted
with Bathsheba.

Let Your mercy dictate
That You grant me
Your grace;
With abundant compassion
My sin, Lord, efface.

Thoroughly cleanse
My iniquity;
Of my sin
Purify me;
Of my transgressions
I am aware;
My sins before me
Are ever laid bare.

Against You alone
I have sinned
And done evil

In Your sight;
Your sentence is justified;
Your verdict
Wholly right.

How true that
With iniquity
I entered this life;
And that
At my conception
My mother's sin
Was rife.
But if You really wish truth
To penetrate my heart
Reveal to me
Your secret lore;
Your wisdom
Please impart.

Purge me with hyssop;
Among the pure
Let me be found;
Wash me,
Make me whiter
Than snow
Upon the ground.

Let me hear
Joy and gladness
On every side;
Let the bones
You have broken
Rejoice far and wide.

From my wrong-doing
Hide Your face;
Remove my sin
That it leaves no trace.

Implant within me
A truly pure heart;
A steadfast spirit
To make a new start;
From before Your Presence
Drive me not away;
Don't remove
Your Holy Spirit;
Within me
Let it stay.

Restore unto me
The joy of Your redemption;
With Your generous spirit
Support my good intention.

Let me instruct transgressors
To walk in Your ways
That sinners might return
To offer You
Their praise.

Save me from bloodshed,
Lord God of my salvation;
To Your righteousness,
Let my tongue
Sing an oration.

Lord, let my lips
Be open wide;
Let my mouth declare
Your praise
With pride.

No sacrifice
Would You have me
Donate;
No burnt-offering

To conciliate.
The sacred gifts
That You seek
Are the humbled spirits
Of the meek;
The broken-hearted
And depressed—
You do not love them
Any less.

Make Zion prosper
Through Your good will;
Build Jerusalem's walls;
All its dreams
Fulfil.

In its sincere sacrifices
You will then
Delight;
With burnt and whole offerings
In Your sight,
And bulls
On Your altar
Offered aright.

Psalm 52

*For the Director. A Maskil-psalm.
For David, when Doeg the
Edomite arrived and said to Saul,
"David has come to Ahimelekh's
house."*

How, O brave one,
Dare you boast
That God's mercy
Is ever extended,
Notwithstanding the evil exertion

That you've ever expended
In the cause of the violence
That you orchestrated
When your razor-sharp tongue
Mischief,
Fabricated?

Far more than
The pursuit of good,
Evil you preferred;
Rather than uttering
Righteous words,
Falsehood
You averred.

You love
To prevaricate;
Deceitful speech
You validate.

But God will ensure
That you're overthrown;
Forever remaining
Desolation-prone;
He'll sweep you away
From your tent
To be wholly disconnected;
From the land of the living
Eternally ejected.

The righteous shall see
And be in awe;
They'll mock him, saying,
"See one so poor
In perception of
God's protective strength
That he would trust
In his own wealth

Thinking he could become strong
Espousing causes
Manifestly wrong!"

But I am like an olive tree
Thriving in God's house;
Belief in God's mercy
I'll ever espouse.

I will ever praise You
For all You have bestowed;
Declaring Your goodly name
To all with faith,
Endowed.

Psalm 53

For the Director. On **Mahalath.**
A Maskil-psalm of David.

"There is no God!"—
The fool thinks
Within his heart;
Corruption and degeneracy
Set men,
From good
Apart.

From heaven
God looks down
Surveying humankind
To find
A discerning man
Attuned to
His own mind.

Sadly
They have all defected;

Impurity
They've all selected;
To do good
Not one elected.

Have those evil-doers
No brains in their head
When they devour my people
As one devours bread;
Never calling on God—
Of faith
Not a shred?

They shall be all
Gripped by fear
When a fearful fate
Is nowhere near!
For God will scatter
All around
The bones of oppressors
On violence bound.
Those You consigned
To eternal shame
You had already rejected
As fair game.

Would that from Zion
Israel's salvation
Might proceed
When God restores the fortunes
Of His people
In need.
Then Jacob shall rejoice
In a manner unrestrained;
And gladness,
For Israel
Shall be reclaimed.

Psalm 54

A psalm with string music. A Maskil-psalm Of David, when the Ziphites came and said to Saul, "Know that David is hiding among us?"

Save me, Lord,
By Your name;
My right,
Assertively
Proclaim.

Lord, please hear
The prayer I utter;
Attend to the words
That I mutter.

For strangers arise
In confrontation;
Assassins seeking
My eradication;
Men for whom God
Is an aberration.

But He shall help me
To succeed;
The Lord's support
Is guaranteed.

He will repay
With an evil fate
My enemies
Who lie in wait;
With the justice

Of His administration
He'll consign them to
Annihilation.

Then I shall present
As a gift to You
A sacrifice
Freely offered;
Praising Your name
For the goodness that
You have always
Readily proffered.

For He delivers me
From all distress;
To my enemies' downfall
I am witness.

Psalm 55

For the Director; with neginoth. A Maskil-psalm of David.

Lord, attend to my prayer,
Do not ignore my plea;
Listen well to my cry,
And promptly answer me
When in anguish
I complain
And moan incessantly
At the clamor of my foe
And the oppressive enemy
Whose evil is aimed
In my direction
With odium
And execration.

My heart trembles
To its core;
Deadly pangs fell me
To the floor;
With fear and trembling
I'm tormented;
Clothed in horror,
Anger
Vented.

Then a thought
Crossed my mind:
With a dove's wing
I'd escape this bind
And fly away
With utmost speed
To reach the refuge
That I need.
To far-off regions
I would roam
Turning the desert
Into my home.

So, let me hasten
To escape the storm
And the slander's
Searing squall;
Confuse them, Lord,
Divide their tongue
For I have seen it all:
City-dwellers' avarice—
All under strife's thrall.
Day and night their mischief
Stalks the city walls,
Within which, iniquity
To injustice
Calls.

Endemic
Is the malice
That within it
Holds sway;
Oppression and guile
From their streets
Just won't go away.
For the one
Who reviled me
Was not an erstwhile foe—
That, I could have borne
As just one more salvo;
Neither was it an enemy
That lauded it over me—
That, I could have coped with
Emotionally.

It was you!
A man
I valued so,
A companion and a friend;
A confidant
With whom I shared
Sweet counsel
Without end,
When on our way
To the Lord's house
With the throng
We would wend.

Men like that
May He lure
To their sudden death;
May they all descend to Sheol
With their dying breath;
For evil
In their home

Resides;
Deep within them
It abides.

As for me
To God I'll call;
He will save
And won't let me fall;
Evening, morning,
And at noon,
When I cry and moan,
I know that He
Listens out
To my every groan;
Rescuing me
Wholly unscathed
From my adversaries
Who outnumber me so vastly
With all their resources.

God overhears
Their dastardly plan;
The Eternal destroys
To a man
Those with no change of heart,
For whom fear of God
Plays no part,
Who'll stab their friends
In the back;
Breaking accords
That were on track.

The flattery of their mouth
Was smooth
While their heart waged war
Against the truth;

The words they spoke
Were softer than oil,
Yet sharp as a sword
Without its foil.

Entrust to the Lord
The burden
You bear;
For He will sustain you
And ever care.

The foot of the righteous
He'll not permit
To falter or to
Descend
To the pit.

But men of blood
And deceit
You, O Lord,
Will defeat;
Into the depths
Of the nether world
You will ensure
That they are hurled,
Before completing
Half their days—
While I trust in You
And in Your ways.

Psalm 56

*For the Director. On Yonat elem
rehokim.
Of David. A mikhtam; when the
Philistines seized him in Gath.*

Have mercy, Lord,
For I'm on the run
From men that persecute;
From adversaries
That all day long
Are in hot pursuit,
Spying on me
With one intent:
Oppression
To execute.

But when I have
Most cause to fear,
To You
I turn in trust;
To the God whose word
I ever praise—
As I know I must.
I will not show myself
Afraid,
For this I truly know:
Mortal man cannot prevail
*If he makes me
His foe.*

Violent words
They hurl at me
Incessantly each day;
I am the focus

Of all their thoughts
In a violent interplay.

They plot;
They lie in ambush;
My every move
They note;
Determined to destroy me,
*With ample cause
To gloat.*

From such an iniquity
Don't let them escape;
In Your wrath
Topple them;
*With ample cause
To quake.*

You, who mark
My wanderings,
Store my tears
In Your flask;
Are they not inscribed
In Your book?—
In truth, I need not ask!

On the day I call
To enlist Your aid
My enemy's treachery
Is repaid;
The clearest sign that God desires
To provide all that
My cause requires.

God will give me cause
For praise;
To His deeds

A toast
I'll raise.

In God I trust
And shall not fear;
What harm can man
Engineer?

Lord, I'm roused
To take on vows;
Thanksgivings I'll pay
To You each day.

For, my life You save
From death's intent;
My feet,
From stumbling
You prevent;
That before my God
I might walk tall
In a life enlightened
By His call.

Psalm 57

For the Director.
Al tash'het. Of David. A mikhtam;
when he fled to a cave
from before Saul.

Have mercy, God,
Be gracious to me;
For to You
As a refuge
I will flee;
A refuge within
Your wings' shade

Until the calamity
Has been allayed.
I call to God
Who is Supreme;
The One
Who fulfills
My every dream.

He reaches out from heaven
To ensure that I am saved;
He denounces my oppressors
As wholly depraved;
With mercy and truth
God's path is paved.

It is as though
I'm made to lie down
Among a lion's pride,
Or strapped to a pyre
With fiery coals inside,
Facing men whose teeth
Are arrows and spears,
Whose tongue is a sharp sword
Ready to pierce.

Be exalted, Lord,
Over heaven above;
Your glory display
To earth's creatures
With love.

They prepare a trap
For my steps
And I am bowed low;
They dig a pit
That I might fall—
But into it
They go!

My heart is steadfast
O my God;
My steadfast heart
Will sing;
And I will chant
A joyful hymn
With all of my being.

Stir yourself
O my soul!
Harp and lyre
Awake!
Let me rouse
The very dawn
For Your glory's sake.

Among peoples
I praise You, Lord;
Among nations
I sing Your praise;
For Your mercy
Spans the heavens,
And Your truth
To the skies
Is raised.

Be exalted, Lord,
Over heaven above;
Your glory display
To earth's creatures
With love.

Psalm 58

For the Director.
Al tash'het.
Of David. A mikhtam.

Muzzled judges:
Can you be trusted
To plead justice's cause?
Can you honestly judge
Ordinary folk
By equitable laws?

Even a mental attitude
Allows injustice to spread,
As if the march to violence
You yourself had led.

On emerging
From the womb
The wicked
Start to stray;
From birth
Liars are known to choose
Their own deviant way.

Like the serpent's venom,
Their own
They purvey;
As an asp
That feigns deafness,
From the upright path
They stray;
As the cobra
That can close its ear
To the charmer's call,
And to the magician's spell

May not respond
At all.

God, smash every tooth
In their mouth
To the core;
Their lion-sized grinders
Rip out from their jaw.

Let them melt,
As when water
Is poured away;
When they shoot
Let their arrows
Fall far from their prey.

Let them melt
As the slug's
Slimy exudation;
As a stillborn that will never see
The sun's illumination.

Before your pans
Have time to warm
From the thorns' flames
Licking their base—
And while the stew
Is still raw
With no cooking interface—
The whirlwind's fury is unleashed,
Destroying
Without trace.

When the blameless victims
All receive
Revenge's recompense,
They will all express their joy

At the end of their suspense;
Bathing their feet
In the oppressor's blood,
To a man, they'll say,
"God is good;
There's reward
For righteous living;
There is a judge of the earth,
And righteousness is winning."

Psalm 59

For the Director. Al Tash'het.
Of David. A mikhtam; when Saul
Sent spies to watch his house
and to kill him.

My God, save me
From all my foes;
Put me beyond the reach
Of all who oppose;
Evildoers,
Let me evade;
As murderers approach
Come to my aid.

For truly
They ambush
My very soul;
Tyrants assemble
To devour me
Whole;
Though no wrong
On my part
Justifies their goal.

Though I have done them
No harm
They choose to accelerate
Violent confrontation
Suffused with hate;
So, rouse Yourself
On my behalf;
Relieve
My abject state.

Indeed, Lord,
God of Hosts,
God of Israel,
Rouse Yourself to punish
All the nations
So they fail;
Keep treacherous villains
Away from
Mercy's trail.

When they return at evening,
Like a dog
They howl;
Around the city
They menacingly
Prowl.

Their mouths utter
Venomous quips;
As piercing swords
They employ their lips;
Not a care do they give
As to who overhears;
Indifferent they are
As to whom
They reduce to tears.

But You will laugh
At their expense;
You'll mock the nations
And their pretense.

The power
You'll wield against them,
I truly wait to see;
For as an impregnable tower, Lord,
You have been to me.

The mercy
God dispenses
Is ever accessible to me;
My enemies' downfall
He enables me to see.
But I ask that
You slay them not
Peremptorily,
Lest it fade from my people's
Collective memory;
O Lord, our shield,
Scatter them
In Your power;
Cast them closer to the ground,
With every passing hour.

Their every utterance
Is a sinful expression;
Their pride will hasten
Their perdition;
For oaths and lies
Are their ready rendition.

In Your wrath
Destroy them;
Remove them

Without trace;
That to earth's end
All might know
That God guides
Jacob's race.

Like a dog
Returning at evening
They'll utter a piercing growl;
Around the city limits
They'll mournfully prowl;
Snooping around
In their search for food;
Famished all night—
In desperate mood.

But I shall hail Your strength
Through the songs that I sing;
Acclaiming each morning
The mercy that You bring;
For You consistently serve
As my reliable tower;
A refuge in my distress
And the source of my power.

Because You are, indeed,
My strength
I'll ever sing Your praise,
As the tower who extends to me
His grace
In many ways.

Psalm 60

*For the Director. Al Shushan
Eduth. A mikhtam of David,
when he fought with Aram-
Naharaim and Aram-Zobah,
and when Joab returned and
defeated twelve thousand
Edomites in the Valley of Salt.*

God, You have cast us off
And breached
Our defensive wall;
After having been
Incensed with us,
Respond now
To our call.

You made earth quake
And cleaved it through;
Now fix its fissures
For its ruin
Is in view.

To the wayward
Of Your people
You showed Yourself
Most harsh;
Delirium-inducing wine
You served
*When they were
Parched.*

But for those
Who truly fear You
An escape
You provide,

Confirming that
Their cause was just
And on You they relied
That those whom You truly love
Would be saved thereby;
So let Your right hand's deliverance
Be Your merciful reply.

God made a sacred promise
That I'd be filled with joy;
That Shechem I would apportion
And Sukkoth's Vale
Deploy;
That Gilead and Manasseh
Would both be mine,
With Ephraim the helmet
Bearing my ensign,
And Judah
Symbol of monarchy
In its prime.

Moab is a pot
In which I shall wash;
Edom, under my shoe,
I shall squash;
Philistia,
How crushed you'll be,
But finally
You'll acclaim me!

Into that fortified city
Would that I were brought
To launch upon Edom
My onslaught!

But You, Lord, chose
to cast us aside;
Deserting our armies—
Victory denied!

Now, therefore,
Against our foes
Bestow much-needed aid;
For worthless is
All human help
Without Your power
Displayed.

Only with God's help
Can we do heroic deeds;
May He tread under foot
Our enemies
Like leaves.

Psalm 61

For the Director. On neginoth.
Of David.

Hear, O God,
My plaintive cry
And to my prayer
Attend;
I call to You
With faint heart
From the earth's
Far end;
To a rock
That is so high
Above my puny reach
Lead me speedily—
For that
I do beseech.

A refuge
You have been to me;
A fortress
Before the enemy.

In Your tent, forever,
Let me abide;
Under Your protective wings
Let me safely hide.

My vows, Lord,
You have noted;
For Your fearers,
A heritage
You have voted.

May you add days
To the king's life-span;
Extend his years
Through generations
Of man.

May he dwell
Before God
For evermore;
Loving-kindness
Employ
To keep him
Secure.

That to Your name, forever,
I may be attuned,
Repaying new vows
That, daily, I've assumed.

Psalm 62

For the Director. On Yeduthun.
A psalm of David.

Truly, my soul
Silently waits
For the God
From whom
Hope emanates.

He is my rock
And my salvation;
A tower, ensuring
I'll never be shaken.

For how long will you stalk
Your fellow man,
Fully focused
On your murderous plan
To crush him
Like a collapsing wall
Or a fence that totters,
About to fall?

Colluding to oust
Those in high position
They resort to falsehood
And derision;
With their mouths they utter
False praise;
In their hearts they curse
Blighting others' days.

Truly, for God
I silently wait;
For from Him

My hope
Shall emanate.

He is my rock
And my salvation;
My tower, ensuring
I shall not be shaken.

My salvation
And my glory
Are for God to dispense;
He is my sturdy rock,
My refuge
And defense.

At all times,
O my people
Give God your trust;
Pour out your hearts
Before Him
Whenever you must;
For He is the only
Refuge for us.

But men veer
To vanity;
Folk embrace
Deceit;
In moral weight
They are mere breaths—
Brief as a heart-beat.

So, trust no venture
That on violence
Relies;
Don't hold your breath
When any enterprise

Involving theft
offers more than expected;
Beware force
For you'll be
Disaffected.

God has said
More than once,
And I've heard it
Reiterated,
That His power
Is paramount
And cannot be
Frustrated.

Kindness
You endlessly dispense;
As reward for good deeds,
Ample recompense.

Psalm 63

A Psalm of David when he was in
the wilderness of Judah.

You are my God
And I seek You out;
Thirsting more than those
Who thirst in drought;
My body likewise
Yearns for You;
No other goal
Will it pursue.

So I sought You
In Your sanctuary—
Glorious strength

Was manifest there—
More precious than life
Is Your mercy to me;
Your praise
My lips declare.

Blessings I shall render to You
So long as I may live;
To Your name
I shall lift my hands
And ardent praise
I'll give.

My soul
Is fully satisfied
Like marrow and fat
Enjoyed;
My mouth will ever praise You
With lips
In joy
Employed.

When on my bed
I reflect
Upon Your Being;
The night-watches
Share my attempt
To probe You,
The All-Seeing.

As a steadfast help
Throughout my trials
You have been to me;
And in the shadow
Of Your wings
I sing confidently.

My soul shall ever
Cleave to You
And where You lead
I'll follow;
Your right hand
Takes hold of me,
And I'll not fear
The morrow.

But those who would
Target my life
To secure its demise,
To earth's depths
Shall be consigned—
Never again to rise.

But if one of their corpses
Is dragged up
By the blade of a plough,
To make a ready meal of it,
The foxes
Will know how.

But the king rejoices
In his God—
All who invoke Him
Are admired;
But the mouths of those
Who utter lies
Shall be permanently wired.

Psalm 64

For the Director.
A psalm of David.

God, hear the sound
Of my voice
Pouring forth my complaints;
From enemy's terror
Preserve my life
As You would that of
Your saints.

Hide me from any harm
That evil-doers
Devise;
From the tumult
Of scoundrels
That villainy,
All prize;
Who make their tongues
Just as sharp
As blades of swords;
As swiftly released arrows
Are all their poisonous
Words,
Aiming at the innocent
From their secret den;
Shooting instantly
With no concern for men.

They encourage each other
In their dastardly designs;
The sole subject they discuss
Is the laying of hidden mines;
Totally confident they are
That no one else will see

Or catch them in the flagrant act
Of their depravity;
Painstakingly they research
The worst iniquity;
Imposing on all involved
Confidentiality.

But God is also
Able to shoot
Arrows suddenly;
Inflicting wounds on the wicked
Devastatingly.

Their own tongues ever utter
Self-incrimination;
All who watch them
Shake their head
In total condemnation.

All tremble
At that sight
And God's righteous deeds
Declare;
Learning from the wicked man's
    doom
To be spiritually
Aware.

The righteous
Shall rejoice in God;
And in Him
Their refuge
Seek;
The upright of heart
Shall exult
Together with the meek.

Psalm 65

For the Director.
A psalm of David.
A song.

To You
Who dwell in Zion
Silence is praise
Well-offered;
To You
In that holy place
Payment of vows
Is proffered.

You are the One
Who attends to prayer;
All flesh approach—
They know
You care.

With the torrent
Of our iniquities
I cannot cope;
That You pardon transgressions
Is our only hope.

Happy the one
You have chosen
And brought close
To Your Presence;
To dwell in Your courtyards
And enjoy the essence
Of the holy spirit
That in Your house resides
And the sanctity that ever
In Your Temple
Abides.

Respond in Your righteousness
And perform wondrous deeds;
O God of our salvation—
Sensitive to our needs—
You bear the trust
Of all mankind
To the earth's end;
To the inhabitants of
The far-off seas
Salvation
You shall send.

By His strength
He founded mountains
Wearing a girdle
Of might;
He stills the roaring
Of the seas
Whose waves pound
And fight;
And the tumult of the nations—
Israel's sorry plight.

Residents of earth's
Remotest nations
Stand in awe
Of Your manifestations;
Lands of sunrise
And sunset
Offer You their exultations.

You favor earth
With much-needed drink
To greatly enrich its yield;
With the gushing water
Of tributaries
You provide corn

In the field;
A covenant with nature
That You graciously sealed.

So, let those soaked furrows seep
Into their ridges below,
Which You soften
With Your showers
And bless
Lushly
To grow.

You crown the year
With goodness
And Your paths overflow
With the richness of the pastures
That abundantly grow.

The desert sprouts
With vegetation;
The hills are girded
With elation.

The fields are clothed
With flocks all feeding;
The valleys wrapped
In grain that's greening;
They shout for joy
And sing
With feeling.

Psalm 66

For the Director. A song.
A psalm

Raise your voice to God
All earth
And sing to His glorious name;
Invest that praise
With a glory
That He alone may claim.

Say to God,
"How awesome are
The deeds
That You perform;
By Your great strength
All Your foes
Are taken by storm;
All the earth shall worship You
And sing aloud Your praise;
Lauding Your name
For many deeds
That ever amaze."

Come and consider all the acts
That God performs;
All uniquely awesome
Transcending human norms:
He turned the sea
Into dry land
That they might cross
Dry-shod;
There we rejoiced
As we walked a path
No man had ever trod.

He rules eternally
By His might;
Keeping the nations
In His sight,
That rebellious ones
Might never unite.

Bless our God
O people;
Let His praise be
On your lip;
He that sustains all of life
Won't suffer our feet
To slip.

God
You have tested us;
Honed us
As silver refined;
Trapped us
And locked our loins
From front
And from behind.

You allowed men
To ride rough-shod
All over our head;
We entered fire and water,
And walked in constant dread—
Though to refreshing waters
We were ultimately
Led.

I shall enter Your house
With burnt-offerings
And repay You
All I vowed:

The utterances of my lips,
The promises
When I was cowed.

Amid the odor
Of burning rams,
Fatty offerings
I shall offer;
Bullocks and goats
I'll prepare,
And my gratitude
I'll proffer.

Come all you God-fearers
And hear me relate
All He's done to reverse
My own sorry fate.

To Him,
My mouth
Called out in prayer;
His exaltedness,
Shall my tongue
Declare.

Had I harbored sin
Within my heart
God would have recoiled
And stood apart.

But God did hear—
He did, indeed;
He responded to my prayer
With speed.

Blessed be He
Who never stood

Aloof from my prayer;
Never did He withhold from me
His Kindness and His care.

Psalm 67

For the Director.
On neginoth.
A psalm. A song.

May God's blessing
Be bestowed with grace;
May we receive the favor
Of His face;
That earth
Might acknowledge
The truth of Your way,
To every nation
Deliverance You display.

Peoples will praise You
O Lord;
Let them all praise
With common
Accord.

Nations will be happy
And sing for joy;
For Your dominion,
Equity
You employ.

You guide the nations of the earth
Earning their praise, O Lord;
Let the peoples continue
To offer You praise,
All with common accord.

The earth has yielded
Produce galore;
May our God
Bless us
For evermore;
Let the earth's far regions
Remain in awe.

Psalm 68

For the Director. Of David.
A psalm. A song.

God shall arise
And scatter His foes;
From before Him
Shall enemies flee;
As smoke is blown
By the wind
You'll banish them
Speedily.

As wax melts
Before a fire
The wicked shall perish
Before God's *ire*;
But the righteous
Shall joyfully celebrate;
Delighting in God
For their happy state.

Sing to the Lord
And praise His name;
Let voices soar
To acclaim
The One who rides the skies
As *Yah—*

Hail His Presence
From afar.

As father of orphans
He furthers the widows' cause;
From His holy place
He surveys them
Without pause.

God houses the homeless
Who are left alone;
Chained prisoners
He liberates
From dungeons of stone;
But the rebellious are lodged
Where to famine
They are prone.

Lord
When You went
At the head of Your folk—
Trudging through desert
To release Israel's yoke—
The earth quaked
And the skies poured rain
At the approach of Your Presence
And celestial train;
At Sinai where
Israel's God
You became.

A refreshing rain
You gifted that day
To revive the spirits
Of those trudging their way
Wearily
Making
Little headway.

A living monument
They were to You there,
When You mercifully provided
For the poor
Ample fare.

When God announced
The victory gained
A throng of our women
With joy unrestrained
Trumpeted the news,
"All enemy kings
Have fled defeated
And from their dwellings
Fellow housewives are rushing
Some spoil to obtain
From what their men
Have removed
From the slain.

"Even you who,
Battle shy,
Hid where the sheep
Lie down
Will claim your doves
With silver-wings
And pinions
Gilded brown."

When Shaddai scattered
The surrounding kings
Far and wide
It resembled Mount Zalmon
With snow on every side.

O lofty Mount Bashan—
You of jagged peaks—
Why do you gaze

With envious eye
At the mount where
The Lord seeks
To make His dwelling permanent—
Mount Zion
From where He
Speaks?

God's myriad chariots
In thousand-fold formation
He occupies
In holiness
As at Sinai's revelation.
You ascended
The lofty heights;
Many captives
You seized;
Tributes from many
There you received;
That it was Your abode
Even rebels
Now believed.

Blessed is the Lord
Our mainstay;
He is our savior
Every day.

God,
We acclaim
As redeemer divine;
He makes death a transition
To a state
Benign.

The heads of His foes
God will cleave;
The hairy skull of those

That treachery
Weave.

The Lord said,
"From Bashan
l shall restore,
As I did My people
Even from the sea floor;
That your feet
May be bloodied
From treading
On corpses
And your dogs' tongues
May relish
Your enemies'
Forces."

The divine king's procession
Crowds shall attend;
When Your way
To the sanctuary
You majestically wend.

Choristers
Will lead,
Then musicians;
Maidens playing timbrels
To new compositions.

Bless God
Amid the great throng;
Let the stock of Israel
Praise the Lord in song.

Young Benjamin
Is prominent there
Instructing
All the guests;

The royal princes of Judah
In their embroidered vests
With the officers of Zebulun
And of Naphtali too,
At the victory procession—
To name but a few.

Your God bids you all
Draw strength
From that which He
Has shown
To the people for whom
He has done so much—
And which He calls His own.

From your Temple
On Jerusalem's heights
Your strength
Is manifest;
Tribute is offered to You
By kings
From North, South, East
And West.

Rebuke the beast
That reclines
By the River's reeds;
The herd of bulls
And their young
For causing stampedes
In the rush to receive their bribes
Paid in silver coin—
So scatter those that delight
In the battles
That they join.

Tribute-bearers
Shall arrive
From Egypt
Bearing gifts;
Ethiopia's emissary
To our God,
Treasure
Uplifts.

All you kingdoms
Of the earth
Sing to God
For all you're worth;
Sing most sweetly
To the Lord;
Invest
With love
Every word
That you direct
To the One who rides
The highest heaven
And ancient skies,
To address
All of His creation
And boom His message
To every nation.

So, acknowledge
The might
Of our God—
Majesty
Manifested;
The entire sky
His strength pervades,
To which Israel has attested.

You are awesome, Lord,
In Your holy place;
Israel's God empowers
By His embrace;
Invigorating a people
Blessed
By His grace.

Psalm 69

For the Director.
Al Shoshanim.
Of David.

Save me, Lord,
For the waters of hate
To my very soul
Penetrate.

I'm sinking into
A deep bog
With no support—
Not even a log!
Plummeting to
The depths of the sea;
A raging flood
Engulfing me.

I'm weary
Of calling out for aid;
My throat is dry
Watching hope fade;
While I wait for my God
My eyes become dim;
My fate turning
Ever more grim.

More numerous are
Those causeless haters
Than the hairs
Of my head;
My would-be assassins
Multiply,
Increasing my dread;
False allegations
In their minds
They have created:
Demanding that I restore
What I never
Misappropriated.

Lord, You know full-well
How into folly
I was drawn;
My sins
Are not concealed from you;
They continue
To spawn.
Let not those
Who wait for You
Be ashamed
On my account;
Let me not add
To problems
That Your seekers
Must surmount.

For it was only
For Your sake
That I was reviled;
That with utter confusion
My face was profiled.

My very own brothers
Accounted me
A stranger;
My mother's sons
Regarded me
An alien
And a danger.

For it was only through my zeal
For Your house
That I was devoured;
By those who reproached You
I was overpowered.

When I cried and gave in
To a regime of fasting,
It only made all their taunts
More bitter and more lasting.

When my clothes
For sackcloth
I exchanged,
They derided me
As someone
Wholly deranged;
They talked about me incessantly,
Those with seats in the gate;
I was the taunt of drunkards—
What lies they'd narrate!

Lord, as for me,
Let my prayer be received
At a time of favor —
Let me be relieved;
In Your great lovingkindness
Answer me;
With sure salvation
Set me free.

Deliver me out of the mire
And let me not sink;
Rescue me from my foes,
From the deep water's
Brink.

Let no floodwater
Sweep me away
Nor depth
Pull me down;
Let no pit's mouth
Seal me in
And claim me
For its own.
Answer me
In Your mercy
Profound;
Show me
A kindness
That knows
No bound.

From Your servant
Don't hide Your face;
Come to my aid
When I'm in
A tight place.

Draw near to me
And redeem my life;
Free me from foes
That foment strife.
You know my reproach,
My shame and disgrace;
You observe all my foes
And my fall from grace.

My heart is broken
By reproach;
I'm sick
With desperation;
Sympathy I sought
From comforters
Was replaced
By alienation.

Into my food,
They secretly poured
Poisonous gall;
For my thirst
They gave me vinegar—
I could hardly breathe at all.

May their own table
Become their snare,
Their trap when they relax;
Dim their eyes
So they can't see;
Make their loins prone
To collapse.

Pour over them
Your indignation;
With fury
Confound
Their situation.

May their settlements
Be laid waste;
In their tents
Allow none
To be based.

Those whom You
Had prosecuted
They pursued
And persecuted;
The anguish of those
For Your faith
Slain
They gloated over
With disdain.

Add that to the sins
They accumulate;
Withhold the mercy
You demonstrate.

From the Book of Life
Let them be excluded;
In the roll of the righteous,
Not included.

But I am afflicted
And much pained;
May Your salvation
Be unrestrained.

I shall praise
God's name
In song;
Magnifying it with gratitude
Upon my tongue.

This will please God more
Than bullocks offered;
Those horned or hoofed,
By humans
Proffered.

When the humble see
My salvation
They are filled
With elation;
God-seekers,
May your spirits soar
With gratitude
Evermore.

For God hears the needy
And their cry;
Those bound to Him
He'll not deny.

Let heaven and earth
Praise Him;
The seas
And all that crawl;
For God shall save Zion
Raising Judah's cities
Tall;
That her citizens
May dwell there
And inherit it all.

The offspring of His servants
Shall possess it with pride;
And all lovers of His name
Therein shall reside.

Psalm 70

For the Conductor. Of David.
For remembrance.

God
Hasten to save me;
Lord
Come to my aid;
Let those who wish
To end my life
Be wholly dismayed;
Let those who seek to harm me
Be confounded and betrayed.

Let all who jeer, "Aha! Aha!"
Be ashamed amid their shouting;
But those who seek You out
Shall have
A joy that's ever mounting;
Let all who seek Your salvation
Ever declaim:
"Magnified be the Lord,
And His glorious name."

Though I am poor
And needy
I am the Lord's concern;
O help and deliverer
Delay not
Your return!

Psalm 71

Lord, Your refuge
I urgently sought;
To shame,
Don't ever
Let me be brought.

In Your righteousness
Save me
And provide redemption;
Listen and implement
Your intervention.

An impregnable habitation
Be to me;
That whenever I need to
There I might flee;
In the past
You have issued
Your command
That to me be extended
A helping hand;
For a rock and fortress
You have been,
Rendering my life
Most serene.

My God,
Redeem me
From the wicked man's
Hand;
From the palm
Of the rogue
And the oppressor's
Demand.

For You remain
My only hope;
From my youth I was sure
You'd help me cope.

From the very moment
Of my birth
On You I relied;
Since You took me out
Of my mother's womb,
Your Praise
I've magnified.

A role-model
I've tried to be
To so many folk;
A tower of strength
You've been to me—
Your name
I ever invoke.
My mouth
Will be filled
With Your praise;
Your attributes,
I'll forever phrase.

Don't cast me away
When I reach old age;
Forsake me not
When my strength fails
Nor abandon me
In my dotage;
Lest my foes
And those that lie in wait
With one accord, say:

"Pursue him!
He has no support!
His God has cast him away!"

Lord,
Be not far from me,
Hasten to help me out;
Let all my accusers
Be ashamed
And suffer
Total rout;
Let those that seek
To harm me
In confusion
Be clothed;
Reproached
By all who know them,
And eternally loathed.

But I shall forever wait,
And praise You
Even more;
Affirming Your righteousness
As salvation's guarantor.

Of all Your mighty deeds
Lord,
I cannot keep track;
When I come to acclaim
The kindnesses
That You never hold back.

You've exhibited
Your wonders
Since I was young;
And until the present day
They are ever
On my tongue.

So, do not forsake me
In my old and gray years;
That I might live
To declare Your power
And open the ears
Of a generation yet to come
That it might desire
To relate all Your mighty acts
To the offspring it will sire.

For Your righteousness reaches
As far as heaven's height;
Who like You
Has performed deeds
So awesome
In my sight?

Though You put me through
　　misfortunes
Beyond compare
You will revive and raise me
From the depths of despair.

You'll invest me
With greatness
And comfort me
All around,
That I'll be moved to thank You
With the lyre's
Sweet sound.
With the backing of
Harp's music
Your truth
I shall declare;
O Holy One
Of Israel,
To You
I offer prayer.

My lips shall never
Be happier
Than when I sing
To You;
The soul
Which You redeemed
Shall join
In praise
That is Your due.

Throughout the day
Your righteousness
My tongue shall acclaim;
But those that seek
To do me harm
Shall be utterly
Put to shame.

Psalm 72

Of Solomon

Your justice, Lord—
I entreat—
Implant within the king;
And with righteousness
Invest the prince
Who will one day
Wear his ring.

That in righteousness
He might judge
Your entire nation;
Your poor
Enjoying justice
With no discrimination.

Let the mountains dispense
To your people
Peace;
Let the hills ensure
That lovingkindness
Shall increase.

He will champion the cause
Of our people's poor;
Protecting the needy
Who beg at the door;
Crushing those that oppress,
And kindness
Ignore.

For so long as sun and moon survive
Your subjects' awe shall also thrive;
Generations handing down
Accounts of the exploits
Of Your crown.

The king's bounty
Shall descend like rain
Falling on a fleece
Or like heavy showers that
To earth
Are released;
That the righteous may flourish
For as long as he reigns
And peace may outlast the moon
When for the final time
It wanes.

May his rule extend
From sea to sea,
From rivers
To earth's extremity;

Desert nomads shall kneel
In submission;
Foes shall lick the dust
In contrition.

Let the kings of Tarshish
And their isles
A handsome tribute
Pay;
Let the rulers of Sheba
And Seba
Bring their gifts each day;
Let every king
Before him
Bow;
Let subject nations
Fealty
Vow.

For to the needy
Who cry out
His aid
He extends,
As he does to the lowly
Who have no
Helping friends.

To the poor and needy
He displays true concern
Bringing to the desperate
The redemption for which
They yearn.

From fraud and lawlessness
He'll ring-fence their lives;
Their preservation
Is prime in his eyes.

So grant the king life
To enjoy Sheba's gold;
Let prayers for him
Be offered
With blessings
Untold.
Let the stems
Of his land's grain
Touch the mountains' peak;
As the forest of Lebanon
With its fruitfulness
Unique.
May his cities' inhabitants
Sprout like country grass;
And all their expectations
May they surpass.

May his name live on
Forever
For as long as sun
Survives;
To endure
And to be invoked
For blessing
In men's lives;
Let nations
Count him happy—
Ensuring that he thrives.

Blessed be Israel's God
Who performs wonders
Alone;
Blessed be
His glorious name;
Forever
It shall be known;
Let His glory fill

The entire earth—
Amen and *Amen*
Intone.

[Here concludes a further section
Of David son of Jesse's psalm collection.]

Book 3

Psalm 73

God is good
To Israel;
The pure of heart
He'll never fail.

My own feet
Almost slipped
And my footsteps
Nearly tripped
When I envied fools
And the peace of mind
That the wicked
Seem to find;
How even in death
They avoid pain
And throughout their lives
Robust remain.

Not for them the toil
Of ordinary folk;
Nor the trauma
Of a mortal stroke;
Instead, as an adornment
They wear their pride;
As a necklace
To be admired;
Violence
They publicly display
As a fresh robe
Donned
Each new day.

Their eyes bulge
From the fat they devour;
On lust

They cogitate
Each hour.

They scoff
And boast
Of their oppression;
Bombastically
Of their aggression.

They target heaven
With obscene lip;
Their tongues
Hold men
In their grip,
Encouraging many
To follow their lead
And to lap up
Their errant creed,
Denying God's knowledge
Of human fate
Or His concern
For man's estate.

Now if those scoundrels
Could be so defiant
And on their success
Blissfully reliant,
If their craving for wealth
They ever satisfy,
Then am I wrong to wonder
Why did I
Clearly in vain
Keep my heart
Pure,
Washing my hands
With virtue's ewer,
Suffering chastisement

With each day's dawn,
Reeling
From Your rebuke
As I rise each morn?

Had I indeed spoken thus,
To Your people
I'd have been
Ruthless;
Had I given credence
To such a thought
I'd have known
That with problems
It was fraught.

But entering
God's sanctuary
The speed of their doom
Was brought home
To me:
Their success
You make
A slippery slide;
That into the abyss
They might swiftly glide.

How desolate,
They are made—
It happens in a flash!
Terrorized
Totally
By falsehood's
Backlash.

Their wealth shall prove
As real to them
As a dream's residue;

That on awakening
From it
There's nothing
To review;
Hence God spurns
The illusion
They seek
To accrue.

My emotions
Were in turmoil;
I felt physically
Shot through;
Crude and devoid of sense
Like a brute
Before You.

Yet my confidence was boosted
Knowing You were near;
When You grasped hold
Of my right hand
Your purpose
You made clear.

So, guide me
With Your counsel;
And at some future hour
Lead me to the glory
That on the righteous
You shower.

For whom have I in heaven
Who cares for me like You?
And on earth I seek no other
To guide me as You do.

Though flesh and heart
May fail me
God shall forever be
The rock on which
My heart relies;
My hope
Eternally.

But they that place distance
Between themselves and You
Shall in an instance
Vanish from view
When You choose to annihilate
The morally askew.

But for me
God's proximity
Shall remain my happiness;
I shall make You
My refuge
And Your deeds
Proudly express.

Psalm 74

A Maskil-psalm of Asaph

Why, Lord, for so long
Do You spurn
Your folk,
And against Your own
Pasturing flock
Such anger
Do You stoke?

Remember Your community
Your ancient acquisition;
The tribe
That You redeemed of old
To give it prime position;
Mount Zion
Your dwelling-place;
Repository
Of Your grace.

With all speed
I beg You view
The lasting desolation
Our foes perpetrated
In Your holy habitation.

Your enemies' roars
Echoed around
Your Temple's meeting-places;
They replaced our symbols
With their own;
Their idols
Filled its spaces.

They were like
Axe-wielders
Against a clump of trees;
Hacking away
At the Temple's carved work
Like frenzied rowdies
Flailing wildly
With hatchet and hammer
And a fury
None could appease.

They ensured that
Your sanctuary blazed;
The abode of Your name
To the ground
They razed.

Fired by the slogan,
"To be annihilated,"
Every place of worship
They located
And throughout the land
Incinerated.

They left no trace
Of our tradition;
No prophets or men
Of erudition.

How long, Lord,
Will You permit
The adversary
To blaspheme;
For how long
Will the enemy,
Your holy name
Demean?

Why do you
Withdraw Your hand
And keep Your right hand
Still?
From Your bosom
Draw it out—
And destroy them
At will.

For You have been my king,
O Lord;
From of old
Showing Your worth;
Delivering Your salvation
Everywhere on earth.

You were the One Who mightily
Divided the sea;
Into its waters
The monsters' heads
You smashed
Mercilessly.

You crushed the heads of
        Leviathan—
That most fearful beast!
Leaving his carcass
For the sea-creatures
As a gargantuan feast.

You cleaved the earth
That it burst forth
With fountain and brook;
Perennial streams
You made dry
With no more than a look;
You brought forth day
As well as night;
Investing sun
With rays
Most bright;
Earth's borders
You delineated;
Summer and winter
You created.

Remember the enemy's
Blasphemous taunt;
Their freedom to spurn You,
The vile ones flaunt.

Surrender not to wild beasts
The life of Your dove;
Fail not Your afflicted
But show them
All Your love.

To the Covenant that we made
Be true;
Earth's dangerous places
Keep under review;
Pastures of violence
Put under curfew.

Let not the down-trodden
Slink away in shame;
Let the poor and needy
Ever praise
Your name.

Arise, Lord,
To pursue Your cause;
Recall the reproach
Levelled without pause
By vile ones showing
No sign of remorse.

Forget not the enemy's
Riotous sound;
The infernal din rising
From Your foes
All around.

Psalm 75

For the Director. Al Tash'het.
A psalm of Asaph. A song.

We praise You, God,
We praise You;
Your Presence
We sense
So near;
Your wondrous deeds
Men acclaim
With an awe
Sincere.

Says God:
"I shall choose the time
To judge with equity;
If earth's dwellers
Are facing doom
I'll extend my pity;
Making its foundations firm
For all eternity.

"I say to scoffers,
'Do not scoff!'
The wicked I warn
Not to show off;
So, issue no challenge
To heaven
On high
O haughty ones
With necks
In the sky.

"*For, no allies shall aid you*
From east or west,

From the desert hills
They'll ignore your request."

God determines
A man's fate,
To demote
Or elevate;
He holds a cup
In His hand
Full to the brim
With a foaming band
Of spiced wine
potent in taste
That the wicked must drain—
None going to waste—
To the very dregs
Till they drool
In disgrace.

But I shall relate forever
How the Lord
Rights wrongs;
To the God of Jacob
I'll dedicate
My songs.

All the pride of the wicked
Shall be eliminated;
But the fortunes of the righteous
Are forever elevated.

Psalm 76

For the Director. On neginoth.
A psalm of Asaph. A song.

God is known in Judah;
In Israel His name is great;
In Salem He sites His sanctuary;
He sits In Zion's gate.

There He smashed
The fiery arrows
Together with their bow;
With shield and sword
He waged His war
And laid His foes low.

Exploding with incandescent light
And gloriously swift;
You swooped down the mountains
Giving enemies
Short-shrift.

Stout-hearted soldiers
Went out of their mind;
Sinking into a stupor
When they could not find
The strength
Even to lift their hands
In their lethargic
Bind.

Horses and chariots
At the rebuke of Jacob's God
Fell into the deepest sleep
Without a single nod.

You are so very awesome;
Who can possibly stand
Before You
When Your anger
Is released
Against a land?

When You pronounce
Your sentence
From heaven
On a nation,
Earth panics
And silence stalks
Every habitation.

When God executes justice
Forever it abides
To save the humble of the earth
Whose destiny it decides.

When fighting men's fury
Yields to a thanksgiving ode;
All lingering wrath
You'll absorb;
To promote
That peaceful mode.

So, vow and pay tribute
All you neighboring states
To the Lord who is your God
And who patiently waits
For men to add their tribute
To the divine store,
Curbing the spirit of princes
And imposing on kings
His awe.

Psalm 77

For the Director. On Yeduthun.
Of Asaph. A psalm.

I raise my voice to God
And cry;
When it reaches You,
With my plea
Comply.

In my distress
The Lord
I sought;
Hand-uplifted
Night-long I brought
My complaint to Him—
It did not cease—
And I could not find
Comfort
Or peace.

When I recall
Times gone by
I moan my sorry state;
I feel so dispirited
When that
I contemplate.

You keep my eyelids open-wide
So that I cannot sleep;
I palpitate
In my fear;
I cannot even speak!

I turn over
In my mind
The events of earlier days,
Of years receding from my mind
When I still earned Your praise.

I recall the joyful songs that
To You
Each night
I'd sing;
Now my thoughts torment me
As I focus on one thing:
Before the Lord
Forever
An outcast shall I be;
Have I forfeited the favor
He used to show to me?

And has His mercy also
Forever been removed;
And the generational promise
With which our spirits
Were soothed?

Has He truly forgotten
How to bestow grace;
Is His anger really so fierce
That His Mercy
It could displace?

I thought again
And realised
It was folly
To reason so:
That the right-hand of the Most
     High
Would deal mercy
Such a blow.

This consideration
Prompted me to recall
The Lord's manifold deeds—
O how I remember them all!
All the wonders
You performed—
Those both great and small.

So, focusing
On all You've done
I'm brought to meditate
That through the holiness
Of Your way
You operate,
Performing deeds no other being
Could ever emulate.

You alone are a God
With wonders to dispense;
To peoples
You have displayed
Strength truly immense.

You redeemed Your people
With incomparable power;
Jacob and Joseph's offspring—
Your nation's first flower.

When the Red Sea waters
Saw You
It was a sight that terrified;
Even the deep was seized by fear—
A miracle
Magnified.
The clouds shed
Their watery load;
The skies

Made a deafening sound;
Once released
Your lightning shafts
Wrought havoc
All around.

Your thunderous indignation
In the whirlwind
Is heard;
Your lightning
Diffuses light
Throughout
The whole wide world.

The earth quakes and trembles;
The sea traces Your way;
Your destination
Through the floods,
A mystery
Will stay.

Like sheep
You led Your people
Mercifully;
Moses and Aaron
Guiding them
To their destiny.

Psalm 78

A Maskil of Asaph.

Attend my people
To my law;
Pay heed to all I say;
My words
I'll preface with a parable

And maxims
Of a by-gone day.

Traditions that
Once they were heard
We chose to internalize;
Thoughts
Our fathers taught us
Culled from words of the wise.

We must not withhold them
From the future generation
But relate the Lord's praise
As a source of inspiration
And His power and the wonders
Performed for our nation.

He ordained this for Jacob
As a testimony to endure;
Entrusting it to Israel
As His sacred law;
With the command to our fathers
That they should transmit
Its contents to their children
As their spiritual remit.

That a body of instruction
From one generation to the next
Might be created—
Handed down
As sacred text;
That their confidence in God
Might proceed with sure steps;
That they won't forget
His wondrous deeds
But keep all His precepts;
Nor follow their fathers—

That stubborn generation,
Rebellious and unfaithful
To the God
Of their nation.

Take the example of
The Ephraimites
Skillful wielders of the bow:
They turned their back
When battle loomed
Without striking a blow.

They did not keep
God's Covenant;
And as for His law—
They refused to walk
In its ways
Or accord to it
Their awe.

They forgot
What He had done for them
And the wonders
He'd displayed
When in Egypt and in Zoan's field
He came to their fathers' aid.

He was the One
Who split the sea
And brought them over
To safety;
Its waters
As a wall
He solidified;
To bring them through
To the other side.

With a cloud He led them
Throughout each day;
A fire's light by night
Showed them
The way;
Flinty rocks
In the desert He cleaved;
Water as if
From the deep
Retrieved;
Droplets
Out of the rock He squeezed;
Water gushed like rivers—
Their thirst
It eased.

Yet their sin against God
Proceeded apace,
Though He was their guide
In that desert place:
To test the Almighty
They devised a plan;
Requesting choice fare
For every man.
Concerning Him
They raised a doubt:
Could He spread a feast
In that place of drought?
Yes, He struck a rock—
Water covered the ground
Forming streams that flooded
The terrain
Around—
But, meat for His people
Could He provide?
A query so faithless
And so snide!

When the Lord heard that
His anger flamed;
A fiery bolt
At Jacob He aimed;
His wrath at Israel
Flared up
Untamed
For not believing
That their God
Could bring salvation
On the nod.

So, the skies above
He notified;
And the gates of heaven
He opened wide;
Raining down on them
Manna for food
And heavenly grain
Generously issued;
Angelic fare
For humans to share;
A provision most plentiful
And most rare.

The east wind He set
On its heavenly course;
The south wind to blow
With its full force;
Flesh
Like dust
Upon them He rained;
More winged-birds than sea-sand
Saw them sustained;
On Israel's camp
He made them alight;
Israel's dwellings marking

The end of their flight.

The people ate
And were satisfied;
That which they craved
He supplied;
But even while
Their mouths were full
They couldn't escape
Gluttony's pull;
So, when God's anger
Over-boiled
He slew their fat ones—
Over-oiled!
And Israel's youth
He despoiled.

Because by sin
They were so seduced
Denying that wonders
By Him
Were produced
He caused their days
To be spent in vain causes,
And their years
In confusion—
With no pauses.

Having suffered deadly
Retribution
They returned to God
In their confusion,
Remembering how
He had been their rock;
Acquitting them
When they stood
In the dock.

But they deceived Him
Having given their word;
Their commitments false
And perjured;
Their hearts
Toward Him
Were not aligned;
His sacred Covenant
They maligned;
Yet He
In His mercy
Pardoned their sin
And did not destroy them
Or their kin.

Often
His wrath
He would suspend;
And all His anger
He wouldn't expend;
Mere flesh
He observed
Merited no concern
As a passing breeze
That does not return!

Often
In the desert
They were prone
To dissent;
In the wilderness
Proving themselves
Insolent.

They provoked God
Again and again;
Imagining

In their limited brain
That Israel's Holy One
They could constrain.

They ignored the times
His hand brought relief;
Ensuring their foes
Could not bring them
To grief:

In Egypt,
His signs
Were fully displayed;
In the fields of Zoan
Were His wonders
Arrayed.

To blood
Each one of their rivers
Was turned;
Undrinkable streams—
With thirst,
Their throats burned;
He unleashed against them
Beasts that devour
And frogs possessed of
Destructive power;
He summoned
The caterpillar
To eat of their yield;
And gifted to locust
The crops of their field;
Their vines
By hail
Were eradicated;
Their sycamores
By frost

Devastated;
Their beasts
By that hail
Were appropriated;
Their cattle
By lightning
Decimated.
All His fierce anger
He released;
Wrath, rage, resentment,
Which never ceased:
A truly deadly delegation,
An avalanche of retaliation;
He plotted His anger's
Trajectory;
Allowing none to escape
Death's victory;
Pestilence blighting
Their destiny.

Every firstborn of Egypt
He put to death;
Their first-fruit
In Ham's tents
Breathed their last breath;
But His own people
He led like sheep;
Guiding His flock
Through that desert
Most bleak;
He led them to safety—
They had no fear;
The sea covered their foes
And their chariot's gear.

To His holy border
His nation He brought;
To the sacred mount
His right hand had sought;
Nations from before them
He expelled;
Settling Israel within borders
Newly-held;
Their tents,
Her tribes
Now occupied;
Reward that their faith
with God was aligned.

But again
The Supreme God,
They tested and tried;
His precepts
Neglected;
His Covenant
Denied

Treachery became
Their primary aim;
As their fathers
Before them—
Objects of shame;
Fickle they were
As a faulty bow's frame.

They vexed Him
With their high places
And idolatrous rites;
Provoked Him
With graven images
And with their sacred sites.

God heard it all
And was incensed
At Israel
Whom He spurned;
He forsook
His Shilo sanctuary
Where
To dwell with man
He'd yearned.

Into captivity,
His might
He sent;
To the estate of foes
All His splendor
Went.

To the sword,
His people
He surrendered;
Enraged
With His heritage,
He was rendered;
His young men
He gave up
To be devoured by fire;
His virgins
Deprived
Of their bridal attire;
By the sword,
His priests
All died;
With shock,
Widows' tears
Instantly dried.

As from a sleep
The Lord
Was roused;
As a warrior
Refreshed,
Having been caroused;
His foes
He drove back
To their ancestral place;
Designating them
A lasting disgrace.

But in Joseph's tent
He declined to dwell;
And Ephraim's tribe
He chose to repel;
Instead it was Judah
Whose tribe He chose;
And His cherished Mount Zion
For His Spirit's repose;
His Sanctuary
Like lofty hills
He erected;
For the duration of earth,
To remain selected.

David
He chose
As His servant
Most loyal;
From the sheepfolds
He took him
To invest him
As royal;
Brought from tending the ewes
To tend Jacob

His folk,
With Israel committed
To bearing His yoke.

He tended them
With steadfast heart;
Guiding them wisely
To a new start.

Psalm 79

A psalm of Asaph

When the heathens invaded
The land You bestowed
They defiled the holiness
Of Your abode;
Inflicting on Jerusalem
Ruination;
With no prospect
Of restoration.

Your servants' corpses
They left as food
For the birds of the skies;
The flesh of Your faithful
They doled out
As wild beasts' supplies.

All around Jerusalem
Like water
Their blood
Was shed;
With none able to attend
To the burial of their dead.

A reproach to our neighbors
We all became;
With scorn and derision
They mentioned
Our name.

For how long, Lord?—
We all asked;
Will Your anger
Forever remain;
For how long
Will Your jealousy burn
Like a fire
Sweeping a plain?

Pour out Your wrath
On the nations
Who treat You
With disdain;
And upon the kingdoms
That refuse
To call upon Your name.

For they've subjected Jacob
To devastation;
And his territory
To annihilation.

Remind us not
Of long-past sins
That we'd rather not face;
Let Your mercy swiftly be restored
For we've sunk
Into disgrace

God of our salvation
Come to our aid;
For the sake of
Your glorious name
That shall never fade;
Save us and efface
All the sins we've perpetrated,
For the sake of Your name
That shall never be
Negated.

Why should the nations
Be enabled to say,
"Where is their God;
Has He gone away?"

When You avenge
Your servants' blood
That on the ground
Was spilt,
In our presence
Those nations
Shall admit
To their guilt.

Let the prisoners'
Agonized cry
Be heard by You
And not slip by;
With the great power
Of Your arm
Free the condemned
From further harm;
But make our hostile neighbors
Suffer seven-fold
For pouring upon You

Blasphemies untold;
While we, Your people—
The flock that you tend—
Will continue to offer thanks
For generations on end;
Declaring Your praise
And assured that You'll attend.

Psalm 80

For the Director.
El Shoshannim.
A testimony for Asaph. A psalm.

Shepherd of Israel
We beg You,
Hear!
You who tends Joseph
As a flock
Most dear;
Enthroned upon cherubim—
We entreat You to appear!

For Ephraim, Benjamin
And Manasseh,
Let Your strength
Be activated,
To secure the salvation
That for them
You have designated.

Restore us, Lord,
To our former state;
By Your favor
Salvation,
Let us celebrate.

Lord, God of Hosts,
Whom we adore
Your people's plea is
For how long more
Will You display anger
And their prayers
Ignore?
You've given them to eat
Tear-soaked bread;
As their drink,
Vast measures
Of the tears
They'd shed;
To our neighbors
You made us
A source of strife;
Among all our foes
Mockery
Was rife.

Restore us
Lord of Hosts
To our former state;
Show us Your favor;
Salvation
Demonstrate.
You uprooted
From Egypt
The vine that You had bred;
Displacing nations,
To plant it there
Instead;
You cleared a space before it;
It took root in the ground;
Its tendrils filling
The land
All around.

Mountains were concealed
By its shadow
So vast;
Mighty cedars were obscured
By the branches it amassed,
Some extending
As far as the sea;
To the river banks
Its shoots showed
Great resiliency.

So why did you demolish
The fences far and near
That passers-by could pluck
Its fruit
Without fear;
That forest boars
Could pull it apart
And creeping creatures
Could gnaw out
Its heart?

God of Hosts,
Return now;
This I do entreat:
Look down from heaven;
Consider well
Your cherished vine's
Defeat.

Recall the stock that was sown
By Your right hand;
And the branch You nurtured
To grow strong and grand,
Now lying burnt
And cut down;
Destroyed with one glance

Of Your reproving
Frown.

So, hold the hand
Of the one at Your right;
Weak folk whom You nurtured
To endow with might.
So that from You
We might never defect;
When we call on Your name,
Sustain *Your elect.*

Lord of Hosts, restore us
To our former state;
Favor and salvation
Toward us, demonstrate.

Psalm 81

For the Director.
Al ha-gittith. For Asaph.

Sing for joy
To the God
Who gives us strength;
To the God of Jacob,
Sing aloud
At length.

Take up the melody;
Beat the drum;
To the sweet lyre and harp
Sing aloud or hum.

Sound the horn for the new moon's
Inauguration;
Though still largely concealed

It marks a celebration:
A statute for Israel
Which Jacob's God decreed,
A testament for Joseph
When appointed to lead
The government of Egypt
Whose tongue had us
Stymied.

Said God:
"From off their shoulder
I've removed a burden—
The weight of a boulder;
Their hands shall no longer
Be constrained
To drag containers
While calloused and pained.

"In distress
When you cried,
Ready relief
I supplied;
From thunder's fastness
I replied;
At the waters of Meribah,
You were scrutinized.

"Take note my people
When I reprimand;
When you submit
By you I'll stand;
No foreign god
With you
Let there be;
Swear no allegiance
To a strange deity;
For I am the God

Who brought you out
Of Egypt
Where you were enslaved;
Open your mouth
And I shall supply
Everything for which
You craved."

But my people
Ignored my voice;
Israel never obeyed;
So I abandoned them
To their stubbornness
And the schemes
After which
They strayed.

If only my people
Would submit;
If Israel would walk
In my way;
I would humble their foes
In an instant;
Adversaries,
With force
I'd repay.

Despisers of God
Shall dwindle away;
To an eternal doom
They shall all fall prey;
But Israel shall feed
On the finest wheat;
From a rock
I'll pour honey
Till you're all replete.

Psalm 82

A psalm for Asaph

In the company of celestial beings
God reigns supreme;
Within His judicial chamber
His judgments
Earn esteem.

For how long
You earthly judges
Will your judgments
Remain unjust;
And will you favor the wicked
And take their word
On trust?

Grant justice to the poor
And protect the fatherless;
Let the afflicted and the destitute
To law,
Have full access.

Rescue the poor and needy
From those who would extort;
Save them from the wicked
And from a biased court,
Whose ignorant judges
Misunderstand the situation;
Whose verdicts are dull-witted
And a threat to earth's foundation.

I mocked them, saying,
"You judges divine,
Though tokens of divinity
To you I may assign,

Know that like ordinary men
You shall also die,
And like princes
To you also,
Failure shall apply."

So, arise, Lord,
As the sole true judge
Of the entire earth;
For the nations are
Your inheritance;
You alone
Assess their worth.

Psalm 83

A song. A psalm of Asaph.

Your silence, Lord,
Do not maintain;
Unresponsive
Do not remain.

For Your enemies
Are in uproar
And Your foes
Toss their head;
To a secret, crafty alliance
Against Your treasured folk
They're led.
"Come," they say,
"Let us cut them off
From the family of nations,
That Israel's name
Be expunged
From international relations."

For their counsel was unanimous:
Sedition with You in their sights;
The tents of Edom and Ishmael,
Moab and the Hagrites.

Gebal, Ammon and Amalek,
Philistia, citizens of Tyre;
Assyria supporting
Lot's offspring—
In an alliance
Of hate and ire.

Do to them as to Midian
And Sisera
In days of old;
To Jabin
At Kishon's brook—
As in Deborah's song
All told:
Meeting their end
At En-dor
Like the fields' dung,
Considered no more.

Rout their nobles
Just as You did
To Oreb and Ze'eb;
To Zebah and Zalmunna's princes,
Dispatched to their grave,
Who said, "Let us seize
Their every possession,
And divide
Their God-given meadows
At our discretion."

My God, please make them
Like dust blown around;

Like stubble which the wind
Sweeps across the ground;
Like a fire which sets
A forest alight;
Like a flame on a hill
Burning everything in sight;
So may You pursue them
In Your tempestuous rage;
Let Your storming fury
Go on the rampage;
Make them so shame-faced
That they seek out
Your name;
Forever abashed and confused
That they perish
From shame.

Then they shall know
That Your name is unique;
Supreme over all the earth—
Man's good
You ever seek.

Psalm 84

For the Director. Al Ha-Gittith.
For the Korahites. A psalm.

Lord of Hosts
How glorious
Is Your habitation;
My soul pines
For Your courts
With anticipation;
My entire being
Singing for joy

At the living God's
High station.

You aid the sparrow in its quest
To find a place to rest;
And the swallow,
For its young,
To build a cozy nest.
That is what
Your altars, Lord,
Have been for me;
O divine king,
They have served
As my sacred
Sanctuary.

Happy are they
Who attend Your house,
Their mouths never tire
Of praise;
Happy the men
Whose strength comes from You
Mentally walking
Your highways:
By Baka's valley
They wend their way
Imagining it a spring;
The early rain clothing it
With an abundance of blessing.

As the pilgrims proceed
On their way
Their excitement intensifies;
To appear before God
In Zion itself
Spiritually revivifies.

Lord, God of Hosts,
Hear my prayer;
Jacob's God attend
And show You care.
God, our shield,
Look with grace;
To Your anointed
Show a gracious face.

Better to be
In Your courts for a day
Than to spend a thousand
In another way;
I'd rather stand at the threshold
Of God's habitation
Than live well in a place
Where the wicked have
Domination.

For the Lord is our sun
As well as our shield;
His grace and glory
Readily revealed;
Never failing to reward
The deeds that the blameless
All record.

Lord of Hosts—
Of this I'm sure—
Happy the man
Whose trust is pure.

Psalm 85

For the Director.
For the Korahites.
A psalm.

Lord, You have displayed
Delight in Your land;
You've restored
Jacob's fortunes
With a mighty hand;
Your people's iniquity
You have forgiven;
To conceal their sins
You've ever striven;
All Your anger
You have suppressed;
Shed the outrage
You once expressed.

Return to us
O God of salvation
And banish forthwith
Your indignation;
Will Your anger at us
Never end;
Throughout the generations
Is it to extend;
Will You not revive us
Once again
That Your folk's rejoicing
May replace its pain?

Your kindness,
We beg You
To display;
Grant us redemption
Without delay.

The Lord God's message
Let me hear:
Peace to the pious—
Life's elixir—
If to folly
They no longer adhere.

For His salvation
Is near to hand;
For them that fear Him
He has planned
A glorious future
In our land.

Then mercy and truth
Will fuse in bliss;
While justice to peace
Will blow a kiss.

From out of the earth
Truth will surge;
Justice
From heaven
Will emerge.

His goodness
The Lord will then bestow;
A bumper yield
From our land
Will grow;
Justice will then
Take the lead;
Forging ahead
At full-speed.

Psalm 86

A prayer of David.

Lord, I beg You,
Incline Your ear
And answer me
Loud and clear
When as poor and needy
I appear.

Keep me safe
For my piety;
Preserve Your servant
From adversity;
You have my trust
Whole-heartedly;
Be gracious
Though I call
Incessantly.

Make Your servant's life
Content,
For to You
Is my soul's ascent;
You are so good,
You forgive with grace
All that petition
In every place.

Lord, I entreat You:
My prayer please hear;
Let my supplications
Ring in Your ear.

I call on You
When I'm distressed
Knowing You'll answer

My every request;
No higher being
To You can compare;
To attempt deeds like Yours
None would dare.

All the nations
You have made
Will assemble before You
On parade;
To worship and to acclaim
The honour due
To Your name.

Greatness
You demonstrate
By the wonders
That You do;
You are a God
Who dwells alone—
And we're reliant
On You.

Teach me Your way
O my Lord
That Your truth
I might pursue;
Focus my mind
Upon the awe
That to Your name
Is due.

Lord, I shall acclaim You
With all my heart;
From honoring
Your great name
I shall not depart.

For Your kindness to me
Has been so great;
You've rescued me even from
Sheol's deepest gate.

Rogues have risen
Against me;
A violent mob
Seeking my life;
They act as if
You were not there—
Their godlessness is rife.

God of mercy,
God of grace,
Long-suffering and kind;
Truth
In abundance
Is the focus of Your mind.

Turn to me,
Be gracious
And grant Your servant strength;
Save the son
Of Your handmaid
And show me at length
A sign of the goodness
I might expect
That my enemies may all blanch
When they reflect
On how You aid and comfort me—
Ever there
To protect.

Psalm 87

For the Korahites. A psalm.
A song.

Zion's gates are adored
Above all Jacob's dwellings
By the Lord;
Men cite the city
Where God lives
In terms that are superlatives.

Rahab and Babylon
I often mention
To friends who have
My attention;
Philistia, Tyre and Ethiopia
Are also all raised
As countries to be singled out
And to be praised;
Their citizens take pride
That they were born there
Because of the great pride
That they all share.
But of Zion
All men
May make the affirmation
That they were indeed born
Within the conurbation
Of the city which the Most High
Determined its foundation.

So, God will acknowledge
In the list of every nation
The empathy with Zion
Of those born at that location.

Every singer
Through his song,
Every dancer
Tripping along,
Says to Zion,
"*You're adored;*
All my thoughts,
To You
Are moored."

Psalm 88

A song. A psalm of the
Korahites.
For the Director.
Al mahalath le'annoth.
A Maskil-psalm of
Heman the Ezrahite.

Lord, God of my salvation,
By day
I cried;
Every night
You saw me
Looking
Petrified.

Let my prayer
Come before You
And attend to my petition,
For I'm overwhelmed
With troubles
And must confront
Sheol's perdition.

Among those destined
For the pit

I'm enumerated;
With those deprived
Of all their strength
I am equated.

Detached from life's discourse
And perceived as the dead;
As the slain
For whom the grave provides
A premature bed;
No longer meriting
Your attention
Or Your caring
Intervention;
You consigned me to
The deepest pit;
In the darkest depth,
Solitary
I sit.

Your fury has flattened me;
Your deluge devastated me;
From friends
You've set me apart;
You made me odious
In their heart;
Ostracized and house-bound,
Eyes red raw
From affliction's pound.

To You, Lord,
I cry each day;
With hands out-spread
As I pray.

Can Your wonders benefit
Those who have died;

Will the shades arise
With praise applied;
In the grave
Will Your kindness
Be affirmed;
In Hades,
Will faith in You
Be earned;
In the darkest regions
Are Your wonders known;
In oblivion's place
Is Your mercy shown?

Hence, to You,
I'm constantly crying;
Each morning
I greet You
With prayer
And sighing.

Why do You spurn me
And conceal Your face,
Dooming me from youth
To perdition's race;
That I think of You
With trepidation
And am overwhelmed
With consternation?

When Your fury
Sweeps over me
It terrorizes
Fatally;
Like a flood
Swirling incessantly
I'm spun around
Mercilessly.

From friends and companions
You have kept me apart;
Into concealment
My comrades depart.

Psalm 89

A Maskil-psalm.
For Ethan the Ezrahite.

To God's loving-kindness
I'll sing endless praise;
To all generations
My voice shall be upraised,
Proclaiming Your constancy
For I can say for sure
That the world
Through loving-kindness
Forever shall endure,
For You dispense faithfulness
From Your heavenly store."

Said God, "A Covenant
With my chosen one
I've made;
To my servant, David,
I ensured it was relayed:
Forever I promise
To sustain your seed;
For all generations
I shall make your throne
Succeed."

Said David
In reciprocation:
"The heavens provide
Confirmation
Of the wondrous devotion
Of Your congregation.
For who can equal our Lord
In the sky;
Or compare with Him
Among the mighty on high?

"On the great angelic council
His majestic awe descends;
To all His celestial circle
The fear of Him
Extends.

"Lord of Hosts,
Who can lay claim
To power
That equals Yours?
Your faithfulness
To all around
Forever
Reassures;
You control
The sea's pride;
You calm it down
When its waves collide;
The monster, Rahab,
Like a corpse You crushed;
Enemies,
To oblivion
Your mighty arm brushed.

"Yours is the heaven,
Yours is the earth;
To the universe
You gave birth;
North and South
You created;

By Tabor and Hermon
You were celebrated;
Your arm,
With power
Is greatly weighted;
Your hand,
With strength
Is permeated;
Your right hand is ever
Elevated;
Equity and justice
Are Your throne's base;
Kindness and truth
Greet You with grace.

"Happy are those responsive
To the trumpet sound;
In the light of Your countenance
They walk around
Rejoicing in Your name
Throughout the day
Elevated by the kindness
That You display;
For You are their strength
And in that they glory;
By Your favor, ours is
A successful story;
You, Lord, have always been
Our most effective shield;
The Holy One of Israel,
As our king
Is revealed."

In past times
To Your pious ones
You conveyed this revelation:
You said,

"I'll help a warrior
Elevate his station;
Exalting one I've chosen
From all others of the nation.

David my servant I appointed
And with holy oil I anointed;
As a sign that my hand
Would be his support
And my arm would be
His strongest escort;
That no tribute
Would any foe extract,
Nor by the ungodly
Would he be attacked;
For, from before him
I'll cut down his foes
And fend off all
His enemies' blows;
But my faith and kindness
I'll ever bestow;
When he calls on My name
Success he'll know;
His borders I'll extend
As far as the sea,
And to the eastern rivers
Shall be his sovereignty;
He will say:
'You're a father to me;
My God and rock
Who has set me free';
And I shall elect him
My firstborn son;
Of earthly kings
Supreme patron.

"Merciful
To him I shall be;
My Covenant enduring
Steadfastly;
My guarantee
Is that his seed
Forever shall remain;
For as long as
The heavens endure,
His throne
They shall retain;
But if his sons
Forsake my law
And my decrees
Do not observe—
If my edicts
They ignore
And from my commands
They swerve—
I shall punish them
With the rod
In return for their transgression;
And for their iniquity
They'll arouse
My worst aggression;

"Yet My mercy
I won't withdraw
Irrevocably,
Nor prejudice
The faith we forged
Immutably;
My Covenant
I'll not profane—
No promise of mine
Is made in vain.

"One major oath
I've taken
By My holy name:
To David
I shall not be false—
Loyal I shall remain;
His seed unto eternity
Shall survive;
Like the sun's heat
His throne shall
Perpetually thrive;
As the moon was created
For eternity,
As a steadfast witness
In the galaxy."

Yet You rejected
And You raged
At Your anointed king;
And that Covenant
You had no qualms
In abrogating;
Dragging his crown
Into the dust—
His honor
Violating.

All the defensive walls he built
You breached with just one blow;
His fortresses You shattered
To the foundations
Deep below;
Passers-by seized pieces
As their souvenirs;
He became the butt of neighbors
And the taunt of peers;
You let his foes raise

Their victorious right hand;
You let all his enemies
Rejoice
Out of hand;
You even bent back
The edge of his sword
Preventing him earning
Victory's reward;
You dimmed the luster
Of his enterprise;
His throne
You hurled to the ground,
Utterly despised;
You shortened the youthful days
Of his reign;
Replaced by an era
Shrouded in shame.

For how Long, Lord;
Will You forever
Remain concealed;
Will Your anger
Burn like fire
In a grassy field?
Remember how short-lived
Is my allotted span;
For what vain purpose
Did You create

The son of man?

Did anyone ever live
Without confronting death;
Can anyone deceive the grave
With his dying breath;
Where are Your mercies, Lord,
That used to be bestowed,
The ones
You promised David
Were genuinely owed?
Remember Your servants
And the taunts they bear;
The derision of countless nations
That leaves me in despair,
Wherewith Your enemies
Have mocked You, Lord,
And the steps of Your anointed
With contemptuous
Accord."

Blessed shall the Lord remain
For all eternity;
We all affirm,
Amen, Amen,
To that certainty.

Book 4

Psalm 90

*A psalm of Moses,
the man of God*

Lord, in every generation
You have been
Our habitation;
Even before
The mountains
Were born
And earth and world
Received their form,
Through eternity
You're the One
Waiting to offer
Divine pardon.

To dust
You consign mankind;
Saying,
"Return O Man;
Leave life behind."

For a thousand years
In Your sight
Are as yesterday
Or a watch in the night.

Men come
Then You sweep them away;
Like a sleep,
So short-lived
Is their stay.
While in the morning
They make hay
Their moment passes
With the day;

In the morning
They all blossom and sprout;
At evening they wither
And become dried out.

For in Your anger
We are decimated;
By Your wrath
Devastated;
Our iniquities
You keep in mind;
Those of our youth
Clearly defined;
For by Your displeasure
Our days are curtailed
And our years vanish
Like a breath
Exhaled.

Seventy years
Is life's allocation;
With the strong enjoying
Some augmentation
To eighty years
To achieve their mission
Which, for most, invites
widespread derision;
As our lives speed
Toward their close
When we fly to
Our eternal repose.

The power of Your wrath
Who can contemplate;
Why do those that fear You
Suffer sorry fate?

Our days,
Teach us to evaluate;
That our hearts,
To wisdom
May vibrate.

Return Lord;
Say when that will be!
And dispense to Your servants
Your sympathy.

Satisfy us with Your mercy
Each succeeding morning;
That we may greatly rejoice
With each new day's
Dawning.

Grant us
In full measure
The supreme joy
Of Your pleasure;
To outweigh the woes
We have known—
Years claimed by pain
As its own.
The fruit of Your deeds
May Your servants enjoy;
On behalf of their children,
Your glory
Deploy.

Let us ever receive
The Lord's grace;
Make our efforts succeed
At a steady pace;
Our endeavors
Establish
Upon a firm base.

Psalm 91

You who find security
In the Most High's
Covert place
And seek protection
Under the shade of
Shaddai's grace—
All I can say
To describe His being
Is that He is my refuge,
My fortress
All-Seeing;
The God
In whom I put my trust
*From birth until
I lie in the dust.*

For He will save you
From the fowler's snare;
From the deadly plague
Striking unaware.

He will protect you
With His wings
That you may endure;
With His shelter as your refuge
You will feel secure;
As a shield and coat of mail
His pledge shall reassure.

Fear no terror
That stalks by night
Or arrow
Released by day;
No plague
That mysteriously spreads
Or scourge

That at noon
May slay.

Though a thousand may fall
At your left
And ten thousand
At your right,
They will not reach
To where you stand
So you might not take fright.

A passive observer you shall be
Of rogues' retribution,
Because you said
Of the Most High,
"You're my secure location."

No evil will befall you;
No plague will approach your tent;
Angels charged with protecting you
At all times
Shall be sent;
They shall bear you aloft
In their arms
Lest you hurt your foot on a stone;
You'll trample on lions and cobras;
Cubs and asps
Shall leave you alone.

"In return for his love,"
Said the Lord,
"I'll be ever by his side;
Whenever he calls upon My name
I'll raise him up with pride;
Let him just call
And I will answer
As troubles appear;
I will protect and honour him

Granting life and good cheer;
Showing him continually
That My salvation is near."

Psalm 92

A psalm.
A song for the Sabbath day.

It is truly good
To praise the Lord;
To sing praises
To the Most High;
To declare Your kindness
At the break of day;
By night
That You're my ally.

To the accompaniment of
A ten-stringed harp
And a lyre's harmony;
With thoughtful lyrics
I'll offer the Lord
My prayerful
Symphony;
For through Your works
I'm filled with joy;
Glorying in deeds
That You deploy.

How great are the acts
You perform;
To a wondrous design
They all conform;
They're beyond the fool's
Comprehension;
The sinner is blind
To their intention.

Though the wicked
May sprout like grass
And evildoers
May flourish,
Their existence is
But short-lived—
No future theirs
To relish.

But You, Lord, are revered
For all eternity;
To the impious
You will ever display
Your enmity.

For they stand
Forever condemned
As Your enemies;
Suffering the direst fate
And the miseries
Of those who are guilty
Of gross iniquity,
Against whom
Dispersal
Is the Lord's decree.

Thus, my pride
Knows no bounds
Like a wild ox
Tossing its horn;
You have anointed me
With the finest oil
As if to royalty
I was born,
Enabling me to preempt

All my wary foes
Deriving satisfaction from
The wicked ones' woes.

But the righteous shall bloom
Like the palm;
As the Lebanese cedar
They'll grow;
Planted firmly
In the Lord's house—
In His courts
They'll overshadow.

In old age
The fruit of their labors
Remains fresh
And full of sap;
Proving that God,
My rock,
Is upright;
Entertaining no mishap.

Psalm 93

The Lord rules;
In majesty
Dressed;
He wears his strength
As a royal vest;
His world's stability
Manifest.

Your throne
From of old
Has remained secure;
From eternity

Your Presence
Served to reassure.

The ocean, Lord,
Raises its voice;
Its sound
Reverberates;
The pounding of
The ocean's waves
Your praise,
Proudly narrates.

Louder than the crash
Of vast seas
And mightier than their waves
Is the way God's glory
Is acclaimed within
His celestial
Enclaves.

The terms
Of Your promises
You rigorously obey;
The holiness
That invests Your house
Is appropriate to Your way;
For all of eternity
Your glory
It shall portray.

Psalm 94

God
Who regards vengeance
As dear,
As God of vengeance
Now appear!

Judge of the earth
Involve Yourself;
Do not remain
Inert;
Accord to the conceited
Their just and full desert.

How long shall the wicked
Have their way
To flaunt themselves
And disobey;
The insolence of evildoers
Passes the test of time,
So why allow them to perceive
Of themselves
As prime?

Lord, consider
How they crush Your folk;
Those close to You
They cruelly choke.

Widow and stranger
Without mercy
They slay;
Orphans
They murder
As if at play;
Saying, "God does not see

Nor does Jacob's God perceive";
They never spare a single thought
For the families left to grieve!

You basest of people
When will you take note;
You fools
When will you learn
It doesn't pay to gloat?
Does the ear's designer
Himself, not hear;
Does the eye's creator
Not see;
Will He not chastise nations;
Man's mentor,
Will He not be?

The Lord knows
Man's inner thoughts
And the vanity
They contain;
Happy the one
Whom You discipline,
To whom Your law
You explain;
Putting him at ease
In adversity
While the wicked
Dig their own pit;
For God will not forsake
His folk;
His inheritance,
He'll not quit.

His verdicts,
With righteousness

Are imbued;
The upright ever affirm
His rectitude.
Against evildoers,
Who will stand
By me supportively;
Opposing all who are immersed
In iniquity?

Had the Lord not come
To my aid
On a bed of silence
I'd have been laid;
The moment my foot
Is about to slip
I'm buoyed up by Your mercy
And supportive grip;
When anguished thoughts
Invade my mind
My spirits are raised
And Your comfort
I find.

With a tyrannical regime
Can one ally;
To make wrong-doing
Lawful thereby?

The righteous man's life
They target as a group;
To condemn the innocent
They triumphantly swoop;
But God has been
My sure tower;
My rock of refuge
Every hour.

Their evil
To their own head
Shall be deflected;
The wicked,
For destruction
Shall be selected.

Psalm 95

Come let us sing
To the Lord
In praise;
To our rock and salvation
Our voices
We'll raise.

Let us seek out
His Presence
And our thanks
Convey;
At the top of our voices
Our praise
We'll relay.

For He is a God
Who is truly great;
Supreme over deities
Who to Him
Would equate.

The depths of the earth
His hand guides;
On the summits of mountains
His Presence
Resides.

His is the sea
For He designed it;
As is the dry land
For His hands
Refined it.

Come let us worship
And bend the knee;
Prostrating before Him
Who made you and me;
For He is our God
And we're the folk in His care;
We are His sheep
And He guides our welfare.

If only today
His demands you'd obey
*And commit yourselves wholly
To His way!*

Don't harden your heart
As at Meribah you did;
At Massah's desert
Where you backslid;
Where your fathers put Me
To the test;
Decrying My works—
Thinking they knew best.

Forty years I suffered
That generation
Dubbing them a heartless
Association
That, of my ways,
Showed no appreciation.

So, in My rage
I took a vow:
"From My haven
They'll be banned
From now!"

Psalm 96

Sing to the Lord
A new song;
Sing to Him
All earth;
Sing to the Lord
And bless His name;
Proclaim daily
The Savior's worth.

Tell the nations
Of His glory;
To the peoples relate
His wondrous
Story;
For God is great
And greatly praised;
His awe
Above all powers
Upraised;
For all the gods
Of the peoples
Are mere imagination;
But the heavens
Came into being
By Divine creation.

Beauty and majesty
Are His emanation;

Strength and splendor
His Temple's foundation.

All you families
Of the nations
Pay tribute
To the Lord;
Glory and strength
Attribute to Him
With common accord;
The glory due
To His Name
Be sure
To ascribe;
Enter His courts
With offerings—
His sanctity
Imbibe.

In the beauty of holiness
Worship the Lord;
Tremble
All you earth-dwellers
Before the One
Adored;

Say to the nations
"The Lord reigns";
As for the world—
He ordains
That from its place
It shall never move;
And its peoples,
With equity
He'll reprove.

Let the heavens exult
And the earth rejoice;
Let the sea and its fullness
Erupt with roaring voice.

Let the fields be happy
And all they contain;
Let the trees of the forest
All sing the refrain:
"Rejoice in the Lord
That He has come
To judge the earth—
And it shall be done;
With a righteousness
Unprecedented;
For its people,
With faithfulness
Cemented."

Psalm 97

The Lord reigns;
Let the earth rejoice;
Many isles shall raise
A joyful voice.

By cloud and darkness,
He is surrounded;
In mercy and justice
His throne
Is grounded;
Fire
From before Him
Emanates;
His foes around
It incinerates.

By His lightning
The world was lit;
The earth watched
And had a fit.

Mountains
Like wax
Before God
Melt away;
Before the One who
Over earth
Holds sway.

His righteous deeds
The heavens
Declare;
To all peoples
His glory
Is laid bare.

Worshipers of images
Were put to shame
As were those that boasted
Of idols
Most vain.
Submit
All you higher beings
To His reign.

Zion heard
And she rejoiced;
Judah's towns
All gave voice
To their joy
That the Lord
Would implement justice

With righteousness
Restored.

For You are supreme
Over everything on earth;
No single higher power
Can match
Your worth.

You lovers of God,
Detest evil-doing!
His pious ones,
He delights
In rescuing
From the hand of the wicked
Who are ever pursuing.

Light is sown for the righteous
Joy for those without blame;
Rejoice in the Lord
You righteous ones;
And His holiness,
Acclaim.

Psalm 98

Sing to the Lord
A new song
For the wonders
He has wrought;
Through His right hand
And holy arm
Victories
He brought.

His salvation
He displayed;
To the nations,

Righteousness
Relayed.

His mercy and fidelity
He would never fail
To activate on behalf
Of the house of Israel;
That to earth's furthest regions
Humankind might see
Our Lord's overwhelming
Acts of victory.

Joyfully shout
To the Lord
O inhabitants
Of earth;
Break forth
Into song
And sing His praise
For all you are worth.

With the harp
Sing your praise
Joyfully to the Lord;
Let the joyful sound of song
Be heard
In harmony with
Harp's chord.

With trumpets
And the horn's sound
Let praise of our regal Lord
Abound;
Let the sea roar
And all it contains;
Let the world and its beings
Utter refrains.

Let the rivers clap their hands
With glee
While the mountains sing
In harmony
Before the Lord
For He has come
To judge the earth—
His Will be done;
Judging with a righteousness
That is beyond compare
And its peoples
With equity
And a quality
Most rare.

Psalm 99

When God holds court
The peoples quake;
Enthroned on cherubim,
Let the entire earth
Shake.

The Lord is great
In Zion;
Above peoples
Raised so high;
Let them hail
Your great and awesome name
As one to sanctify.

In his love of justice
Our King's strength
Lies;
You created equity;
Truth wears

No disguise;
Justice and integrity
You made Jacob's prize.

Magnify
The Lord, our God;
To His footstool
Bend the knee;
Recite the declaration:
"Holy is He!"

Moses and Aaron
Among His priests;
Samuel
Who called on His name;
When they cried out
To the Lord
His response swiftly came.

In a pillar of cloud
He spoke to them;
His decrees
They observed;
immutable statutes
He imposed;
But they were never
Unnerved.

Lord, God,
You responded to them;
Forgiving,
As was Your pleasure;
But their misdeeds
You avenged,
Exacting measure
For measure.

Acclaim the Lord
As our God
While you bend the knee
Before His holy mountain,
For a most holy God
Is He.

For the Lord is good,
And His steadfast love
Forever prevails;
To every generation
Devotion
He Unveils.

Psalm 100

A psalm of thanksgiving

Call aloud
To the Lord,
You who inhabit
His world;
Serve Him with joy
And approach
With happiness
Unfurled.

Recognize
That our God
Is the One
Supreme;
He made us—
So we are His—
The sheep of His pastures
Green.

Enter His gates
With thanksgiving;
Let His courts echo
Your praise;
Give thanks to Him
And bless His name
*With your hands
Upraised.*

Psalm 101

Of David. A psalm.

Of mercy and justice
Let me sing;
The gift of my song
To You
I'll bring.

In integrity's way
Let me be schooled;
When
By it
Shall I be ruled?
Let innocence of heart
Be my chosen way
That within my home
It may be my mainstay.

At an unseemly sight
Let me not glance;
Scoundrels
I hate
And shall give them
No chance;
Let unworthy thoughts
Stay out of my way;
Over me let evil
Hold no sway.

Against him that slanders
In secret
A friend,
My destructive powers
I shall send.

I cannot bear
The haughty-eyed
Or hearts puffed up
With misplaced pride;
I seek out the trusted
Of the land
To sit with me
At hearings
Planned.

The man of integrity
Alone shall merit
To serve me;
He that devises
Devious schemes
Shall find no shelter
Under my roof's
Beams;
He whose speech
Is full of lies
No advancement
Shall realize.

Against the wicked of the land
A mortal battle
I'll wage;
Ridding God's city of evildoers
My anger
I'll assuage.

Psalm 102

A prayer of the distressed,
When about to faint,
And before the Lord,
Pours out
His complaint.

Lord, accept
My plea of contrition;
Keep the way clear
For a petition.

Hide not Your face
In my time of stress;
To my plea
I beg You acquiesce;
When I cry out
Swiftly respond;
Confirmation
Of our bond.

For, like smoke
My life is speedily spent;
My bones like coals
Burn away;
And I'm left shriveled
And withered like grass
Neglecting food
Every day.

My bones protrude
Through my skin
That my ceaseless wailing
Has made so thin;
I've come to resemble
The desert owl

Or the small owl
On waste land;
An inquisitive sparrow
Alone on a roof,
Its next destination
Unplanned.

My enemies taunt me
The entire day;
Mockery and curses
They hurl
My way.

I eat ashes
In place of bread;
My strong drink diluted
By the tears I've shed;
Because of Your wrath
And indignation,
Your rejection of me
In Your vexation;
My days
As lengthening shadows
Pass,
And I just wither
Like the grass.

But, You, Lord, dwell
For eternity;
Each age acclaiming
Your divinity.

You will rise and be kind
To Zion again,
For that merciful era
Has dawned;
The time appointed

For the release
Of those
That for her
Have mourned.

For Your servants delight
In her every stone
And love every speck
Of her dust;
Prompting nations to fear
The name of God,
And kings
In Your glory
To trust.

For, when God arrives
To rebuild Zion
As the place for His glory
To dwell
He shall answer the prayer
Of the tamarisk—
That knows loneliness
So well.

Then Israel's prayer
He will not reject
But His response
Will be inscribed
For those generations
Yet to come
Who will praise
The redemption
Prescribed.

For the Lord looks down
From His holy height;
From heaven

Keeping earth
In sight;
Listening out for the groans
Of the incarcerated
To free those
Who for death
Were designated;
That in Zion
His name
May be acclaimed;
In Jerusalem,
His praise
Proclaimed;
When peoples and kingdoms
In common accord
Shall all assemble
To serve the Lord.

While still in my prime
He weakened my strength,
And the days of my life
He reduced in length;
Though I pleaded,
"My God
Don't take me away
In mid-life
But let me stay;
You Who all generations
Span
Let my welfare be part
Of Your eternal plan.

"Long ago
Earth's foundations
You alone laid,
And the heavens
By Your divine hands

Were, with wisdom, made;
Yet while they may perish
You'll remain;
As a robe
They'll wear out
But You'll be the same;
Like a suit
You'll exchange them
Erasing their name.

But You are there
Eternally,
And Your years
Roll on
Interminably.
Let Your servant's offspring
Dwell secure;
Let their seed
Be established
And long endure."

Psalm 103

For David.

O my soul,
A blessing of the Lord
Declaim;
With all my being
Praise His holy name;
O my soul,
A blessing of the Lord
Declaim;
All His kindnesses
Do not disclaim:
How He pardons the sins
You perpetrated

And heals all your sick
And debilitated;
How from the pit
He redeems
Your life;
With His loving embrace
Protects you
From strife;
How countless blessings
He bestows
When life is in its bloom,
And how He renews your youth
Much like the eagle's plume;
How He performs
Righteous acts
And justice
For the oppressed;
Revealing His ways to Moses
In response to his behest;
Performing for Israel
Great deeds
At their request.

Compassionate and gracious
Is the Lord;
Long-suffering is He
With mercy
Out-poured.

He will not tolerate
Strife
Unending,
Nor permit a grudge
To remain
Pending.

He does not respond
As our sins deserve;

Our iniquities
He does not conserve.

For, as distant as heaven
Above the earth
So is God's kindness
To His men of worth;
Just as He made east
Far from west
He'll make our sins so remote
That they're not assessed.

Like a father's compassion
For the offspring he sired
Is God's mercy
To those who
With awe
Are fired.

For He knows that our passions
Cannot be contained;
That we are as dust
Finely grained.

As for man,
Like grass are his days;
As the flower of the field
He thrives
To amaze;
Before the wind appears
And blows it away,
Leaving no trace
Of its display.

But God's loving-kindness
Shall never depart
From those

Who show Him awe;
And their righteousness
Shall accrue
To that which their offspring
Store;
Reward for their commitment
To the Covenant
Agreed;
And for their fulfilment
Of all that God decreed.

In heaven
God established His throne;
Exercizing dominion
All alone.

Bless the Lord
O angels on high;
Mighty beings that comply
With His bidding and obey
His every word
Without delay.

You heavenly hosts
Bless the Lord;
You who attend Him
With common accord.

Bless the Lord,
All you
Whom He made,
Wherever His dominion
Is displayed;
Bless the Lord
O my soul,
Created within me
To make me whole.

Psalm 104

Bless the Lord
O my soul;
Lord, You're uniquely
Great;
Attired in glory and majesty;
Yet attuned to man's
Lowly estate.

You wrap Yourself
As with a cloak
In primordial light;
The heavens
You spread
Expansively
As a curtain
Dazzlingly bright.

Rafters
In the waters above
He created;
For heaven's loftiest chambers
Designated;
As His chariot
The clouds
Were employed;
On the wings of the wind
Transported and buoyed;
Messengers
Out of the winds
He made;
Fiery flames enlisted
As His aid.

He founded earth
On a secure base;

Never to be moved
From its place;
The deep
You created
As earth's cover;
Above mountains
You made
The cloud-waters hover.
From Your rebuke
Those waters fled;
From the crash
Of Your thunder
Rushing away
In dread.

Mountains rose
And valleys sank
To levels You dictated;
Impassable boundaries
For the seas
You designated;
That earth would never become
Wholly inundated.

You caused spring-water
To gush forth
To make the rivers swell,
And between the mountains
Find a way
For the tasks
You compel:
For the beasts of the field
To drink their fill;
For wild asses to slake
Their thirst at will;
For birds who make

Their nests nearby
And from among the foliage
Chirp to the sky.

You water the mountains
From Your lofty stores,
Feeding earth in ways
Uniquely Yours;
Making grass spring forth
As food for cattle,
And plants
Requiring man's toil;
To extract his food
From the earth
After he's tilled
The soil.

Wine gladdens the heart
Of man;
Oil makes complexion
Bright;
Bread sustains
Human life;
It is our staple
Bite.

The trees
The Lord has planted
All drink their fill,
Making Lebanon's cedars
Grow taller still;
Attracting birds to their branches,
There, to make their nest;
The cypress tree a home where
The storks
May take their rest.

High mountains are home
For wild goats;
In crags
The rock-badger
Hides;
He made the moon
For seasons;
When to set,
The sun decides;
When You bring on the darkness
Night reigns supreme;
Then all beasts of the forests
Have their own regime:
The lions roar for their prey;
Seeking food from God
Without delay;
But at sunrise
They withdraw;
To stretch out and snooze
On their lair's floor.

Then it is
That man goes out
To pursue his work;
Laboring hard until dusk
At tasks
He doesn't shirk.

How numerous, Lord,
Are the things You've made;
All with wisdom
Overlaid;
Earth teeming
With Your creatures;
All endowed
With unique features:
There's the sea

Vast and wide
With innumerable beings
That swim and glide;
Living things
Small and great—
Some splashing wildly,
Some sedate.

There go the ships
Sailing along;
Passing Leviathan
Immense and strong
Whom You created
As an object of sport—
The rest all expect
Their food to be brought
By You precisely
When it is sought.

You do indeed provide it,
And they're all supplied;
Your bounty ensuring
That they're satisfied.

But were You once
To hide Your face
It would terrify;
Were You
To withhold their breath
They'd instantly die;
To the dust
They'd be returned
Where forever
They would lie.

But were You to
Restore Your spirit

They'd be born again;
So, hear my prayer
And grant renewal
To all the world's terrain.

May the Lord's glory
Endure forever;
May He rejoice
In His creatures'
Creative endeavor.

Just one of His glances
At the earth
And it will quake with fear;
Just one touch
Of the mountains
And clouds of smoke
Appear.

So, while I live
let me sing
Joyfully
To the Lord;
Throughout my days
Let me sing His praise
To show
How He's adored.

May my meditation
To Him be sweet,
That my joy in God
May be complete.
May sinners
From the earth
Be banned;
Let the wicked
Vanish
By His command.

Bless the Lord
O my soul;
Let us praise Him
And extol.

Psalm 105

Praise the Lord
Call on His name;
Among the nations,
His deeds
Proclaim.

Sing to Him
Let Him be praised;
Tell of His wonders
With voice
Upraised.

Take pride in
His holy name;
Let all who seek Him,
To joy
Lay claim;
Seek out the Lord;
His power
Explore;
Intercede with Him
Forever more;
Recall
The wonders
He has done;
Signs of His love
And judgments won
For the seed of Abraham,
His servant
Most true;

For Jacob's offspring,
The chosen
Few.

He is our God—
That is for sure;
Surveying all—
Both rich and poor;
The Covenant with them
He ever recalls;
For a thousand generations'
Protocols,
Which he signed
With Abraham,
And to Isaac
He swore;
Confirming
To Jacob
That it would endure
As a Covenant for Israel
For evermore,
Saying,
"The land of Canaan
To you I grant—
An allotted heritage
And perennial plant."

That was when
Their number was few;
A handful of settlers—
A nation's debut—
When they'd wander
From one nation
And arrive at the next;
In each and every kingdom
Susceptible to be vexed.

But He suffered none
To oppress His folk;
Punishing kings
For imposing
Their yoke;
Saying,
"My anointed
Don't dare to confront;
And my prophets
"Don't dare to hunt."

Famine,
He summoned
To stalk the earth;
Bread's staff
He broke,
Creating dearth;
Ahead of them
He sent a man:
When Joseph was sold,
Slavery began.

They placed his feet
In fetters;
With irons
He was confined;
Till his prediction
Was fulfilled
And God's promise
Refined.

The king commanded
His freedom;
The ruler
Secured his release;
Appointing him over
House and estate

To manage with expertise;
Authorized to restrain courtiers
As he saw fit,
And to instill into elders
Both wisdom as well as wit.

Hence Israel came
To Egypt;
Jacob dwelt
In Ham's land;
God made them multiply
And more than their foes,
Expand.

They made of God's people
An object of hate;
Contriving for God's servants
A violent fate.
So He sent Moses His servant
And Aaron whom He chose
To display signs of His power—
In Ham's land
Wonders
And woes.

He dispatched a darkness—
Intensely dark;
Not a single plague
Failed to find its mark;
All their water
He turned to blood;
The fish decaying
In the putrid mud;
Teeming frogs
Overran their land;
In the royal chamber
Things got out of hand;

Again, He spoke—
Swarms of insects
Appeared;
Throughout their borders
Lice *leered*!
In place of rain
Hail
He sent;
Flaming fire
To their land,
Hell-bent.

He smote their vines
And their figs;
Their country's trees
He smashed
Into twigs;
Another command,
And locusts were sent;
Then countless grasshoppers
Everywhere
Went;
Every herb in the land
They consumed;
The fruit of the soil
They totally doomed;
Every firstborn in their land
He struck down;
The first fruits of their vigor;
Of their joy,
The very crown.

With silver and gold
Israel went on its way;
Not a single tribe
To misfortune
Fell prey;

The Egyptians rejoiced
To see them go;
For fear had gripped them
On account of that foe.

Over them He spread cloud
As a protection;
For their night-vision,
A fire's reflection;
At the people's request
He showered them with quail;
Heavenly food
With no travail;
He split a rock
And water gushed out,
Flowing as a stream
On land parched
by drought.

He kept to the letter
Of the Covenant He'd made
With Abraham, His servant,
To his offspring conveyed;
So He brought out His folk
With a joy most profound;
His chosen ones
With gladness
Were all crowned.

He gave to them
The lands of nations
And tributes raised
By annexations;
That they might observe
His teachings and laws;
And sing *Halleluyah!*
Without pause.

Psalm 106

Halleluyah!:
Praise the Lord
For He is truly good,
And all His loving-kindness
The test of time
Has stood.

The mighty acts
Of the Lord
Who can declare;
Of all the praise
He deserves
Who can make folk
Aware?

Happy are they
Who justly act
And always do
What is right;
Remember me, Lord,
When You favor Your folk,
When You save them
Keep me in sight;
That I might prosper
With Your chosen ones,
Sharing the joy of
Your nation;
Feeling a profound pride
In Your people's
Vindication.

We sinned
Just like our forebears,
Straying and doing wrong;
When in Egypt

They discounted
Your wonders
Though timely and strong.

Neither did they remember
The abundance of
Your love,
But rebelled at the Red Sea
Against the One Above.

Yet He continued
To save them
As befitted His glorious name;
Unfailingly
Displaying His power
To their eternal acclaim.

The Red Sea,
He rebuked;
It dried up
Instantly;
Dry like a desert
The deep became;
When He led them through
Safely.

From their foes
He delivered them;
From their enemy
He set them free;
Water covered their adversaries;
Not one reached
To safety.

Then they believed
His promise,
And in their song

He was hailed;
But speedily
They forgot His deeds
And spurned the plan
He unveiled.

In the desert
They gave in
To their lust;
In the wasteland
Put God to the test;
But He struck them with
A wasting disease,
After granting
Their request.

There was widespread envy
Of Moses
Throughout the camp;
And of Aaron
His brother
Who bore
God's holy stamp;
The earth opened
And swallowed
The arch-rebel
Dathan,
And covered the defiant rabble
Of his brother
Abiram;
Fire enveloped
Their faction;
By its flames
Were the wicked
Devoured;
A calf
They made

At Horeb;
A molten image
With deity
Endowed;
Their glory
They surrendered
For the image of a bull;
One which devoured grass
By the bellyful.

The God
Who saved them
They denied;
He whose deeds
In Egypt
Had been their pride;
He'd performed wonders
In Ham's land;
At the Red Sea, wonders,
Supremely grand.

Were it not for Moses
His chosen envoy,
God's decision
Would have been
Swiftly to destroy;
But he leapt
Into the breach
To ensure God's wrath
Wouldn't reach
To destroy the people
He'd impeached
Because they'd rejected
The desirable land
And dismissed His appraisal
Out of hand.

In their tents,
Their complaint
They refined;
God's voice
They shut out
Of their mind.
So, by way of oath,
He lifted His hand
That in the desert
He would disband
Them and their seed
To be absorbed and scattered,
And by nations and lands
Bruised and battered.

To Baal Peor
They attached themselves
And on it they doted;
Partaking of sacrifice
To the dead
As those fervently devoted.

They provoked anger
By that deed;
A plague He unleashed
Spread with speed.

Then Phinehas stepped in
To intervene,
Dispelling the plague
With an ardor most keen
That was attributed
To His merit,
And throughout the ages
To His eternal credit.

At the waters of Meribah
They provoked once again,
Making Moses suffer
Incomparable pain
When they rebelled against him
And he spoke with disdain.

The indigenous nations
They didn't destroy;
A deed God said
That they had to employ;
Instead, with the nations,
They mingled at will;
All their decadent acts
Content to fulfil:
They worshipped their idols
And by them were ensnared;
To offer their offspring
To demons,
Prepared;
Innocent blood
They casually shed;
Sons and daughters' blood
To Canaan's idols
They fed;
Polluting the land
With the blood
Of the dead;
By such acts
They became defiled;
Debauched by behavior
Most vile and wild.

God was incensed
With His people;
His inheritance
He abhorred;

He surrendered them up
To nations,
To be ruled by
An enemy horde;
Their foes
Oppressed them sorely;
Subjecting them
To their power;
Though He saved them
Frequently
Their rebelliousness grew
By the hour;
To the extent that
By their iniquity
They were humbled
And made to cower.

Then He reviewed
Their bitter distress
And paid close heed
To their cry;
Confirming to them
The Covenant
He'd committed Himself
To apply;
A measure of divine remorse
Enabling their captors thereby
To reconsider and look at them
With a merciful eye.

Deliver us
O Lord, our God;
Gather us
From among the nations,
To acclaim Your most holy name
And to praise You
In orations.

Blessed be the Lord,
God of Israel;
To all eternity
He will prevail.
Let all the people
Say, "Amen";
Halleluyah!
Let them all hail.

Book 5

Psalm 107

"Praise the Lord
For He is good;
His kindness,
The test of time
Has stood."
So say those
Redeemed of the Lord
Whom He has delivered
From the enemy's *sword*,
Whom He in-gathered
From various lands:
East, west, north, south,
And their myriad clans.

Some in desert and wasteland
Strayed;
With no settled place
For a home to be made;
Hungry and thirsty
Their spirits depressed,
They cried to God
When they were distressed,
And He offered relief
To the oppressed.

A city for settled residence
He directed them how to find;
And they thanked the Lord
For His steadfast love
And His wonders
For mankind.

To those who were thirsty
Ample drink He supplied;
And those who went hungry,
With fine fare He plied.

Some were confined
To the darkest deep
And bound by irons
Most cruel;
Because they defied
The word of God
And spurned
The Most High's rule.

Through the most bitter suffering
He humbled their heart;
They stumbled
Unaided,
Despised and apart.

They cried to God
When distressed;
He relieved them from
That which oppressed;
From deepest darkness
They emerged
Into light;
The chains that bound them
He snapped
In His might.

So, let them offer
Thanks to God
For being gracious and kind;
And for the many wonders
He performs
For humankind:
For the bronze doors
He shattered
And the iron bars
He smashed;
Fools

For whose errant ways
And for other sins
He thrashed;
Their food
All tasting loathsome
As to death's gates
They were lashed.

They cried to God
When distressed;
He gave them relief
From that which
Oppressed;
Issuing an order
That they be healed;
That the decree of the pit
For them be repealed.

So, let them offer
Thanks to the Lord
For being merciful and kind,
And for the many wonders
Performed with man in mind;
Let them offer sacrifices
Of thanksgiving
And relate with joy
All the deeds
Performed *for the living.*

There are sea-faring men
Traveling far in ships,
Crossing great oceans
On their business trips;
Men who've seen many
Of the Lord's deeds
And the wondrous nature
Of the deep

That from Him
Proceeds.

A whirlwind was raised
By His word
Whose waves surged
Angrily;
Up to the heavens
And down to the depths
Engendering misery;
They reeled and staggered
As a drunkard
Abandoned by their skill;
They cried to the Lord
In their distress
And He alleviated
Their ill.

He reduced the storm
To silence;
And the waves
He made quite still;
The passengers relished
Their calm return
To the destination
Of their will.

So let them offer
Thanks to the Lord
For being merciful and kind,
And for the many wonders
He performs
With man in mind;
Then men shall exalt Him
Wherever they congregate
And praise Him where the elders
Assemble in the gate.

He transforms rivers
Into arid ground;
Where springs abounded
Thirsty land is now found.

Once-fruitful areas
He converts
Into salty marsh;
For all its inhabitants
Making life
Most harsh.

Out of deserts He makes pools
Gushing water to excess;
Springs of water He creates
Out of wilderness.

There He settles the hungry
To develop where they live;
Sowing fields and planting
    vineyards
And, through initiative,
Yielding a fruitful harvest
And a life most productive.

Hence the blessing
Of the Lord
And hence their increased yield;
No animal will they lose
While grazing in the field.
All this in contrast to the time
When they were few and crushed;
By want, sadness, and sorrow,
Totally ambushed.

On men of rank
He pours contempt

And makes them lose their way
In a desert waste—
No guiding track—
Where they were sure
To stray.
The upright shall see this
And they shall rejoice
When wrong-doing, forever,
Shall lose its jarring voice.

Whoever is wise
Will take note
And on God's lovingkindness
He will dote.

Psalm 108

A song. A psalm of David.

My heart is loyal
And to you
A song I shall sing;
Praise I shall offer
From my inner being.

O harp and lyre,
To music
Awake!
While I rouse
The dawn
For His glory's sake.

I shall thank You
Among peoples;
Among nations
Sing Your praise;
For Your kindness

Transcends heaven;
With Your truth
To sky
Upraised.

Be exalted
Over heaven above;
Your glory
On earth
Display now
With love.

So Your loved ones
May be rescued
Be prepared to save;
Answer and deliver
With Your right hand
Most brave.

At God's sacred promise
I was filled with joy:
That Shechem I would apportion
And Sukkoth's Vale
Deploy;
That Gilead and Manasseh
Would both be mine
With Ephraim the helmet
Bearing my ensign,
And Judah the essence
Of monarchy in its prime.

Moab is a pot
In which I shall wash;
Edom, under my shoe
I shall squash;
Over Philistia I'll emit
A triumphant shout

Heralding to all around
Her total rout.

Into fortified cities
Who shall lead me on,
Ensuring my war with Edom
May be decisively won?

But have You not
Cast us aside
Deserting our forces—
Victory denied?
Now is the time
To bestow Your aid;
When man's help
Is vain
Like every promise
Made.

Only with God's help
Come victorious deeds;
For He will tread
Under foot
Our enemies
Like leaves.

Psalm 109

For the Director.
For David. A psalm.

God, to whom I offer praise
Be not deaf
To my cries;
For the tongues
Of wicked and deceitful men
Against me

Pour out lies.

With words of hate
They encircle me;
They attack me
Without cause;
They repay my love
With hostility
Though I prayed for them
Without pause.

Every favor
I do for them
Elicits an evil retort;
Any love
I display
They viciously distort.

Appoint a rogue as accuser
At my enemy's right hand;
That he may be found guilty
When he takes the stand;
And let any plea that he makes
Meet with reprimand.

May his days
Be limited;
To his estate
Let another succeed;
Make his children
Orphans,
And his wife
A widow
Bereaved.

Let his children
Be vagrants
Forever begging food;

From their hovels
Seeking out
Morsels to be chewed.
All his possessions
Let the creditor
Seize;
Let strangers plunder
His goods
With ease.

To him
Let no mercy
Be extended;
To his orphans
No guardian
Recommended.

Let his offspring suffer
Devastation
And his name cut off
From the next generation.

Let his father's iniquity
Loom large in God's mind;
Let his mother's sin remain
Clearly defined;
On God's record inscribed
For eternity;
But from earth
Erased forever
Shall their memory be;
Because acts of kindness
Had no place in his mind,
And he hounded to death
The deprived and maligned.

Because he loved to curse,
The curse bounced back;
Because he mouthed no blessing
It took a distant track;
So may that curse be like
The uniform he wore;
Like water may it be absorbed
Into his core;
Or like the oil
That soothes one's bones
When they are sore.

Indeed, let that curse
As his own cloak remain;
As a favorite belt
Worn time and again.
Thus, may God repay
All my accusers;
May all who speak ill of me
Be permanent losers.

But You, Lord,
Act for me
As befits Your Name;
In Your kindness and mercy
Save my life,
Assuage my pain.

For I am poor and needy,
With a heart
Pierced to the quick;
I fade as a waning shadow
Or a locust
Swat
With a stick.

From fasting,
My knees caved in,
And my body fat
Has all waxed thin;
An object of scorn
I have become;
Those who see me nod
With tedium.

O Lord, my God,
Come to my aid
And mercifully save;
Then all shall know
That my release
Came by Your Hand
Most brave.

Curse, they might,
But You will bless;
Those who oppose me
Shall have stress,
While to joy
Your servant
Shall gain access.

A cloak of confusion
May my accusers don;
Make them wear their disgrace
Just like a robe
Put on.

To the Lord
My mouth shall sing
Abundant praise;
Amid a throng
My voice I'll raise.

For, by the right side
Of the needy
He will always stand,
To save him from all who would
Condemn him out of hand.

Psalm 110

Of David. A psalm.

The Lord spoke
To my lord, *the king,*
Saying, "Sit at my right hand,
While I make your foes
Your footstool—
Obedient to your command."

Your scepter's rule
Beyond Zion,
The Lord will extend;
With the promise:
"Your dominion
Over foes
Shall never end."

On the day
You declared war
Your subjects volunteered;
Those who
Not long before
Had from the womb appeared;
In all your majestic holiness
They came to offer to you
The sacred years of their youth
With its distilled dew.

The Lord has sworn
And won't relent:
"Be My priest forever;
As the rightful king—
You have my word—
*I'll support
Your best endeavor."*

The Lord is at your right hand
Crushing kings when enraged
And judging all the nations
With whom you are engaged;
Piling up bodies
Crushing heads
Far and wide—
*Creating devastation
With every single stride.*

But the king will drink
Fresh water
From a brook
Along the way;
And walk with pride
Knowing that
God is his mainstay.

Psalm 111

Halleluyah!,
I'll praise the Lord
Wholeheartedly,
Before the upright
At their assembly.

The Lord's works are truly great
And when they are required

He speedily ensures that
They're readily supplied.

With splendor and glory
His acts are performed;
With boundless generosity
They're forever informed.

For His wondrous deeds
He has won renown;
Grace and compassion
Are the hallmarks of His crown.

Food for those who fear Him
He readily supplies;
The terms of His Covenant
He forever applies;
The power of His deeds
To His folk
He relates
When granting them
The nations' estates.

Truth and justice
Are His sole deeds;
His precepts
Faithfully
Relate to our needs;
Steadfast
They shall remain
For eternity;
All formulated
With truth and equity.

Redemption He sent
To His people in need;

An enduring Covenant
He guaranteed.

Holy and awesome
Is His name;
Ever deserving
Of our acclaim.

Wisdom's foundation
Is fear of the Lord;
All who possess it
Have deep insight
Assured;
His praise
For eternity
Is secured.

Psalm 112

Halleluyah!
Happy the man
Who fears the Lord
As best he can;
Who is wholly committed
To His will
And plan.

Mighty in the land
His offspring shall be;
An upright clan,
Blessed
Generously.

Riches and wealth
In his home
Shall abound;

The effects of his virtue
Shall forever be found;
For the upright,
A light
In the darkness
Shall shine;
Grace, mercy and virtue
In him
Combine.

Fortune shall smile on him
Who lends generously
And conducts all his affairs
With total equity;
Never shall he be evicted;
His righteousness
Shall ever be depicted;
He need have no fear
Of a malicious report,
But be confident
Because the Lord
He sought;
With resolute spirit
He'll not agonize;
But be a spectator
Of his foes' demise.

He that gives generously
To the poor—
His merit
Shall ever remain;
He shall be honored
And his success
Shall never be on the wane.

When the wicked see
They'll be vexed

And gnash their teeth
With spite;
At the thwarting of their desires
They'll lose the urge
To fight.

Psalm 113

Halleluyah!

All you servants of the Lord
Let His name be praised;
For ever and ever
Let it be blessed
With voice strongly upraised;
May the name of God
Be greatly praised
From the sun's rising
Until its light fades.
All the nations
The Lord transcends;
Beyond the heavens
His glory extends.

Imagine
One Who dwells as high
As God
Embracing
The meek and shy;
Descending
To evaluate
Heaven's and earth's
On-going state;
Raising the poor from the ash
And the needy from the heap of
    trash,
To sit with princes of the realm

Or supervisors
At the helm!

The childless woman
Within her home
The Lord installs,
As a happy mother
Blessed with young,
Responding to their calls;
May Halleluyah! thanksgiving
Resound around your walls.

Psalm 114

When Israel left Egypt's land,
Its language
Jacob's clan shed;
Judah was dubbed
A tribe set apart;
God's dominions
Israel led.

At the approach of the Israelites
The sea looked and fled;
The Jordan churned backwards
In a maelstrom of dread;
The mountains skipped about
Like rams;
The hills frolicked
Just like lambs.

What is it
That alarmed you, sea;
What is it
That made you flee;
Why, Jordan,
Did you flow back,

Or the mountains skip
Like rams;
And why O hills
Did you frolic
Just like frisky lambs?

From before the Lord
Tremble O earth;
From the presence
Of Jacob's God,
Who turned the rock
Into a pool
Though wielding no rod;
A flowing fountain
From flinty rock—
He released
On the nod.

Psalm 115

Not for us, Lord,
Not for us,
But for Your name
Grant glory;
That Your love
And Your faithfulness
Might adorn
Our nation's story.
Why should the nations
Have cause to say,
"Where is their God
Has He gone away?!"

Not so—
Our God,
In heaven

Remains;
What He delights in
He sustains.

Their idols are
But silver and gold
That men have made
And then extolled:
A mouth they have
Yet cannot speak;
Eyes
But cannot see;
Ears they have
Yet cannot hear;
A nose
Without ability
To savor aromas
Discerningly;
Hands they have
Yet cannot feel;
Feet
Yet cannot walk;
Though endowed with a throat
Its sounds
Don't resemble talk.

Those who make them
Shall become
Just the same—
Inert;
As will those
who trust in them
And miraculous traits
Assert.

But you, Israel,
Trust in the Lord—

He is their help and shield;
O house of Aaron
Trust in the Lord—
As their warrior
He's revealed;
You God-fearers
Trust in the Lord—
Your security will be sealed.

The Lord will keep us
In His mind;
Bestowing blessings
Of every kind:
He will bless the house
Of Israel
And Aaron's dynasty;
He will bless those
Who fear Him
And acclaim His majesty;
For small and for great alike
He's their divine trustee.

May the Lord
Increase your numbers—
Yours and your children's too;
May you all be blessed
By the Lord
Who made heaven and earth—
And you!

The heavens belong
To God alone;
The earth
He gave to man;
The dead cannot praise You—
That was never His plan;
Neither can they who descend

Into the silent nether world;
Only *we* may bless Him
Till eternity is unfurled.

Offer Halleluyah! praise;
Let your voices be up-raised.

Psalm 116

I love the Lord
For He listens out
To my petition
And to my shout;
Whenever I call
He inclines His ear;
When all around
Is death's frontier;

When Sheol's torments
Single me out;
When I suffer troubles
And sorrow's clout,
Then I invoke
The name of the Lord,
Pleading for my life
To be restored.

The Lord is gracious;
He is just;
In His compassion
I put my trust;
The vulnerable
He protects;
When I am desperate
He reconnects.

So, be at rest
Once more,
My soul;
For the Lord's response
Will make you whole.

For You released me
From death's grasp;
My tears
You have dried;
My feet
From stumbling
You have saved;
My enemies
You've defied.

In the lands of the living,
Before God
I'll walk tall;
Confident in my faith
And though about to fall;
Having said in my haste—
Perhaps ungraciously —
That all men are conditioned
To speak untruthfully.

How could I be worthy
Of God's generous reward?
The cup of salvation
I raise to the Lord;
Invoking His name,
That's so adored.

My vows to God
I shall repay
In the sight of His nation;

For I know that when the pious die
There's divine consternation.

O Lord,
I am Your servant
Your handmaid's son;
You released the chains
That bound me
And restored my freedom.
So, a thanksgiving offering
I shall offer You
And invoke Your divine name—
As I was ever wont to do.

My vows to the Lord
I'm ready to pay
In the sight of His people
Assembled to pray
In Jerusalem's courts
Of the Lord's abode—
Listen out for
The Halleluyah! ode.

Psalm 117

Praise the Lord
All nations;
All you peoples
Hail His name;
For His mercy
Is unbounded,
With truth
His eternal claim.
Halleluyah!
Let everyone exclaim.

Psalm 118

Praise the Lord
For He is good;
His kindness
Shall ever endure;
Of this,
Israel, Aaron's seed,
And God-fearers
Are sure.

I called on the Lord
In my distress;
He answered me
With largess.

The Lord is with me;
I have no fear;
What possible hurt
Can men engineer?

With the Lord
Serving as my support
I'll see my foes
In their own trap
Caught.
Better to trust
In the Lord above
Than in any human's
Professed love.

Better to take refuge
In the Lord
Than in nobles
With motives
Unexplored.

Though many nations besiege me
With hostile intent;
In God's name
I'll cut them down
Till my anger is spent.

They have indeed besieged me
With hostile intent;
In God's name
I cut them down,
Till my anger
Was fully spent.

Though they besieged me
Like a swarm of bees
They perished as fast
As dry trees,
Devoured by a sweeping
Conflagration
When I beseeched God
For their annihilation.

You foes—
When you thrust me forward
To make me fall,
The Lord was there
To help me;
My doom
To forestall.

The Lord is my strength
And my song;
He'll remain my salvation
Now and life-long.

In the tents of the righteous
Are victorious songs of joy;

Recounting the exploits
He called His right-hand
To deploy.

Triumphant
Is the Lord's right-hand;
His myriad victories
Swift and grand.
I shall not die—
I shall live for sure,
To relate God's deeds
All great and pure.

Though chastisement
Was His just decree,
From death
He mercifully
Spared me.

O gates of mercy
Open wide;
Let me enter
To praise Him there
With pride.

This gate is sacred
To the Lord Above;
The righteous enter
With spiritual love.

I praise You
For having answered me;
For being my Savior
Devotedly.

The stone
That the builders disdained,

Cornerstone position
In the Temple
Attained.

All this
God contrives;
It is truly wondrous
In our eyes.

The glorious day has arrived
When God's will is done;
Let us exult and rejoice
At the victory
We have won.

Lord, we beg You save us
From violent visitation;
Lord, let our efforts meet
With successful realization.

Blessed is
He that comes
With God's mission
In mind;
From the house of the Lord
He shall receive
A blessing
In kind.

God
The source of our light
In our festive offerings
Takes delight;
To the altar's horns,
They are bound,
With cords
Secured
All around.

You are my God,
To whom thanks
Are due;
You are my God,
And I'll acclaim
You.

Thank the Lord
For He is good;
His mercies
The test of time
Have stood.

Psalm 119

Those whose way
Is blameless
Who in God's law
Walk proud
Reflect
The inner happiness
With which
They are endowed;

Those who cherish
His doctrine
Seeking Him
With all their heart
Discover an inner happiness
That shall never depart.

Acts of injustice
They cannot do
For they are fully focused on
His path *of virtue.*

Your laws were issued
By Your command;
Total obedience
Is Your demand.

Would that my conduct
Was firmly directed
To observing Your laws,
With none neglected!

Then I'd suffer
No flush of shame
Reviewing the commands
Issued by Your name.

I'll praise You
With a sincere heart
As I learn
Your righteous laws;
Because I keep Your decrees
Do not forsake my cause.

∾

How may a youth
Be sure to maintain
The upright way?
Obedience to Your word
Will ensure he'll never stray.

I pursued Your commandments
With every good intention;
Aid my desire never to be drawn
Into their contravention.

Your words are cherished
In my heart;
To sin is unthinkable
On my part.

Lord, to Whom
All blessings are due
Teach me the laws
Revealed by You.

All the rules
That You created
My lips have
Enunciated.

Far greater joy have I derived
From what You decree
Than from the acquisition of
Some costly luxury.

On Your precepts
I meditate;
Toward Your paths
I gravitate.

In Your laws
I find delight;
I won't forget
Even one insight.

∾

Deal kindly
With Your servant
That I may be spared
To keep all the precepts
That You have declared.

Open my eyes
That I might discover
Wisdom more wondrous
Than any other.

My stay is fleeting
At this earthly abode,
So, withhold no commands
Still to be bestowed.

My soul unceasingly
Swoons with desire;
With love for Your precepts
It is afire.

Justifiably cursed
And insolent men
You subject to condemnation;
They stray so far
From Your commands,
Bringing shame to our nation.

Shame and contempt
Remove from me,
As I attempt to observe
All You decree.

Though princes may conspire
To ruin my reputation
Your servant engages
In sacred meditation

Your laws and precepts
Are my sole delight
And my close companions
By day and night.

&

My soul clings
To the dust;
Revive me

As You said
You must!

When I sought Your aid
To find my way
You promptly replied;
So, instruct me now
In Your precepts
And be ever by my side.

The principles of
Your commands
Let me comprehend;
Let me meditate
On Your wondrous acts
*Which continue
Without end.*

I am wholly
Racked with grief;
As You promised,
Grant relief.

Keep me from following
A false direction;
Let Your teaching be
My inspiration.

The path of faith
I chose as my own;
Your rules,
For my life
Set the tone.

To Your precepts
I've ever cleaved;
Don't shame me, Lord,

Or leave me grieved;
That the way of observance
I might pursue,
For You broadened my mind
As my insights grew.

∾

Teach me, Lord,
The way of Your laws
And I'll observe them forever
Without pause.
Let me understand them from
A sound perspective,
That I may fully cherish
Their objective.

Guide me along
Your commandments' way
For over my life
They hold sway.

Direct my heart
To Your law's embrace,
Rather than to any
Monetary chase.

From falsehood's allure
Divert my eyes;
Let my safety be
Your enterprise.

Your promise
To Your servant
Keep,
That all who fear You
Reward,
Might reap.

Remove from me
The reproach
I dread;
Let Your goodly laws
Bring joy instead.

Your precepts
I passionately desire;
In Your mercy provide
All I require.

∾

May Your kindness
Envelop me;
May Your promised salvation
Appear;
Then I shall rebut
All who taunt;
For Your word
I revere.

Let not my mouth be at a loss
For a cogent reply
While I await the vindication
*That I pray
You won't deny.*

Your teaching
I shall ever obey
*With my loyalty
Prominently on display*;
I shall walk around
With a carefree air
For I judge Your precepts
As beyond compare.

Emboldened I'll be
To address kings
On the wisdom of
Your law;
For my delight
In Your commands
Increases more and more.

Therefore I reach out to
Your cherished commands
And meditate fervently
Upon all Your demands.

～

Remember the promise
To Your servant
That inspired me with hope;
My comfort in affliction—
You enlivened me
When You spoke.

Though I suffered
The cruelest taunts
Of arrogant folk,
I never once departed from
Your law's benign yoke.

For my comfort I rely
On Your precepts revealed
In times gone by.

The wicked cause me to be seized
By a fierce rage,
When I witness how
From Your law
They disengage.

Your laws
Transform where I dwell
Into a place of song
Where all is well.

I invoke Your name, Lord,
In the night
And commit to Your law
With all my might.

This comfort has been
My reward,
For with Your law
I was in accord.

～

That the Lord is my portion
Is my proud claim;
To abide by Your word
Is my constant aim.

Whole-heartedly,
Your favor
I have sought;
So show me the grace that
Your word has always brought.

With the righteous way
I've been occupied;
Directing my feet
To Your precepts' side.

I made haste
And did not delay
To keep Your commandments
And never to stray.

Though the bonds of the wicked
Coiled me around
It was to Your law
That I remained bound.

At midnight
I rise
To offer You praise
For Your righteous precepts
Which refine my ways.

To all who fear You
I am a friend;
To Your laws
They zealously attend.

The earth abounds
With Your mercy, Lord;
Teach me Your statutes
Let me reap reward.

∽

Your servant's welfare
You've always pursued;
Through Your promise,
*With confidence
I was imbued.*

Discernment and knowledge
Teach me well;
For Your laws I affirm
*And in them
I excel.*

Before I suffered
I went astray;

Now I act
Just as You say.

You are good,
And good You do;
Teach me the statutes
Emanating from You.

The arrogant have chosen
To smear me with lies;
But observing Your law
Makes me energized.

Their heart
Like fat
Has become crass;
But my joy in Your law
None surpass.

I was content to have been
Afflicted by You
That I might learn from Your law
To pursue virtue.

More precious to me
Is the law of Your lips
Than thousands of gold
And silver *chips.*

∽

Your hands made me,
And my growth
You oversaw;
Now motivate me
To study
Your law.

Those that fear You
See me and rejoice,
Knowing my desire
To obey Your voice.

I always accepted
Your just decisions;
And the justification
Of all Your afflictions.

May Your indulgence
Put my mind at rest
As Your promise to me
Made manifest.

Only by Your mercy
Do I enjoy existence;
For Your law is my delight
As well as my subsistence.

Let the insolent
Be ashamed
To distort my way
Through lies;
But meditating
On Your law
Makes me
Profoundly wise.

May Your loyal ones
Support me
Out of knowledge
Of Your decrees;
May I follow Your laws
Steadfastly;
And may all my turmoil
Cease.

❧

For Your salvation
My soul pines;
I wait patiently
For Your word
And for all
That it enshrines.

For Your promise
I am bleary-eyed;
Wondering when comfort
Will be applied.

Though parched
As a skin bottle
Shriveled by smoke,
My pledge to Your sacred law
I'll never revoke.

How long may Your servant
Expect to live;
When will You punish pursuers
Who take me captive?

The insolent
That defy Your law
Have dug pits for me;
Your commandments are true;
Without cause they pursue—
Offer me Your security.

Though they almost
Removed me
From off the earth,
To not a single precept
Did I give a wide berth.

Preserve my life
In Your steadfast love
That I may keep the laws
Handed down from above.

∾

As the heavens are immortal
So are the words of Your law;
Your faith is for eternity;
Earth's launch
You oversaw.

Men commit to Your edicts
This day,
For they wish to serve You
In every way.

Were it not
That Your teaching
I cherished,
In my great affliction
I would have perished;
So I'll never neglect
Your precepts
Which have kept me alive;
I'm Yours
Because I followed Your law—
So ensure that thereby
I shall thrive.

On me
The wicked focused
To secure my destruction;
But my sole preoccupation
Was with Your instruction.

Of material things,
I've observed
Their innate obsolescence;
But Your infinite commands
Are immune—
As is Your very essence.

∾

My love for Your law
Is truly great;
On it I love
To meditate.

Your commandments
Make me wiser
Than all my foes;
They enable me
To avoid
Any threatening woes.

More than
All my teachers
Insights I have gained;
For Your precepts
Challenged me—
Their appeal never waned.

More knowledge
Than my elders
I accumulated;
For Your commands
I perceived
As eternally mandated.

Every path to evil
My feet sought to evade;

Faithful to Your instructions
I have ever stayed.

From Your precepts
I have not departed
Because of the instruction
That You imparted.

How more pleasing to my palate
Are the precepts You prescribe
Than the sweetness of the honey
That my lips imbibe.

The wisdom I've gained
From Your instruction
Makes me hate false schemes
As paths to destruction.

∾

Your words serve
As a lamp to my feet;
As a light for the path
*That will make me
Complete.*

I took an oath
That I must fulfil:
To observe the laws
That reflect Your will.

Because I'm afflicted
In every way;
Preserve me
As promised
Without delay.

Accept the offerings
I have gifted;
Teach me the rules
That ensure
I'm uplifted.

Though my life is in danger
At every turn,
Not for a moment
Your law
Did I spurn.

When the wicked
Laid a trap
For my feet,
From Your law
I never beat
A retreat.

My eternal heritage
Were Your laws;
Of the joy of my heart
They were
The cause.

My heart's desire
Was to fulfil Your law
For as many years
As I had in store.

∾

I cannot stand
Double-dealing,
But for Your law
I have
A loving feeling.

You are my shelter
And my shield;
My hope lies in
Your word
Revealed.

You evildoers
Keep your distance
That my Lord's commands
Meet no resistance.

Support me
As You promised
So that I might live;
Make no attempt to frustrate
My initiative.

Sustain me
That I may be saved;
To explore Your laws
I ever crave.

Those that spurn Your decrees
You reject;
Falsehood and deceit
They project.

You banish the wicked
As dross to be shed;
Hence my love for Your law—
The crown for my head.

Because of my fear of You
My body starts to quake;
I remain in awe of the demands
That Your edicts make.

❧

All I've done
Has been just and right;
Save me from those who plan
For me a sorry plight.

Assure Your servant
That success will be mine;
Let not the arrogant
Oppress me all the time.

My eyes are sore
From seeking
Your salvation;
For when Your promise
Wins verification.

Deal with Your servant
As Your kindness demands;
Teach me to value
All Your commands.

I am Your servant;
Make me appreciate
The nature of the precepts
That You dictate.

The time has come
To act for the Lord;
For Your sacred law
Has been ignored.

Your commandments
I rightly adore
More than the very
Finest gold in store.
Hence it is

That Your law
I've always used
As the measure for that which
With equity
Is suffused;
Thus, I shun
Every false way,
Knowing how easily
One may stray.

∾

Your decrees are wondrous—
Each one I internalize;
You begin to speak
And light floods forth
To make the simple wise.

I open my mouth wide
And pant with desire;
For I long
For Your commandments
Which set my soul
On fire.

Turn to me
And display Your grace—
As You ever do—
To all lovers of Your name
Who render to it
Its due.

Make firm my feet
As You promised
That no evil
May hold sway;
Preserve me

From oppression
That Your precepts
I might obey.

Show favor
To Your servant;
Your precepts
Teach me well;
My eyes shed
Streams of water
For Your laws
Which men repel.

∾

Lord,
You are so righteous
And Your rulings
Wholly just;
Righteous decrees
You ordained;
On faith
They are focused.

I am consumed with zealous rage
When I see my foes ignore
Your words so perfectly refined
And that I so adore.

Though I'm lowly
And despised
Your precepts
I don't neglect;
Your righteousness
Is eternal;
Your teaching
Just perfect.

Though distress and anguish
Come my way
Your commands
Are my delight;
Your righteous decrees
Are eternal—
Let me learn
To live upright!

∽

When I call out
With all my heart
Answer
Without delay;
That I may continue
To observe Your laws
Loyally
Each day.

When I call on You
Save me
That I may live by
Your decrees;
When I rise before dawn
And cry for help,
For Your promise
I offer pleas.

My eyes pre-empt
Each night-watch
As Your words
I review;
In Your mercy
Hear and revive me,
As You always do.
Those addicted

To vulgarity
Are all close to hand;
Remote from Your teaching
They form a sorry band.

But You share
My proximity;
Your laws exude
Integrity.

I knew from the outset
On surveying Your laws
That they were enduring—
Every phrase and every clause.

∽

Consider my affliction
And rescue me,
For I've never neglected
Your law;
Champion my cause
And redeem;
The life You promised,
Secure!

Salvation eludes the wicked,
For Your laws
They never sought;
In Your abundant mercy
Revive me
With the justice
That You wrought.

Those that pursue me
And persecute
Have greatly multiplied,

While from Your instructions
I've never turned aside.

When I see defectors
I feel disgust;
In Your promise
They put no trust.

Lord, see how Your precepts
I embrace;
So, revive me with the kindness
You readily put in place.

Truth
You prioritize;
Your Just law
Forever applies.

∾

Princes pursue me
With no justifiable cause;
But at Your word
My heart beats fast
Without a single pause.

At Your word
I rejoice
Beyond all measure;
As one who
Unexpectedly finds
A considerable treasure.

Falsehood I hate
And abhor;
My love is reserved
For Your law.
Seven times daily

I offer You praise
For Your righteous instruction
Which refines my ways.

Those that love Your law
Enjoy peace of mind;
Never shall they be misled
Nor maligned;
For Your deliverance
I patiently wait
Fulfilling
Your commands
In a holy state.

Your precepts
I readily
Take to heart;
All my love
To them
Do I impart.

Your laws and precepts
I obey;
Before You
My deeds
Are on display.

∾

My plea
Receive with favor,
Lord;
Your promised insights
Now accord.

Allow my petition
Before You to ascend;
To Your promise to save me

It's time now to attend.
Let my lips pour forth
Appropriate praise
As thanks for teaching me
Your ways.

To Your promise
My tongue
Shall testify;
For on Your just commands
We all rely.

Stretch out Your hand
To aid me,
For Your laws
Are my sole choice;
I long for Your salvation
For in Your teaching
I rejoice.

Grant me life
That I may offer praise;
Let Your precepts
Guide me
Through life's moral maze.
I strayed
Like a lost sheep;
Search for me
I pray;
I did not neglect
Your commands,
But ever did obey.

Psalm 120

A song of ascents

To God I called
In my distress;
He answered me
With largess.

Lord, save me
From treacherous lips;
From a deceitful tongue
And its cruel quips.

How do you propose to benefit;
What do you expect to gain?
Because of your deceitful tongue
All you'll reap is pain:
Warriors' sharp arrows
In juniper coals made hot;
To dwell with Meshekh
In Kedar's tents—
Has been my sorry lot!

Among haters of peace,
For too long
I've resided;
But when I seek to negotiate,
On war
They've decided.

Psalm 121

A song for ascents

My eyes are raised
To the hills;
From where will help arise?

It will come from God
Who made heaven and earth
His creative enterprise.

He'll prevent your foot
From giving way;
Your guardian won't sleep
For a single day.

The guardian of Israel
Will neither slumber nor sleep;
He'll be your guardian
So as to keep
You protected
And to serve as a shade
At your right hand
So you won't be afraid.

The sun shall not
Harm you
As it beats down by day;
By night
You'll not suffer
The moon's hostile ray;
He'll ensure
That from evil
You'll be protected;
Guarding you zealously
So you won't be
Affected.

He'll watch over you whenever
You leave or return;
From now and forever
You're His chief concern.

Psalm 122

A song of ascents. Of David

When friends said to me,
"To the Lord's house
Let's be going,"
My response was a sense of joy
Akin to overflowing.

O Jerusalem
Our feet have stood
Within your hallowed gates;
The now rebuilt Jerusalem
Is a city
That integrates.

There the tribes ascended—
All blessed by the Lord—
A testimony for Israel,
To His name
Thanks are out-poured.

There
The judges' thrones
Were placed—
The thrones of David's line;
Pray for the peace
Of Jerusalem:
"May your lovers
At ease recline;
Within your ramparts
May peace ever reign;
May your citadels epitomize
Tranquility's domain."

For the sake of my kin
And all my friends,

For your well-being
I pray;
For the sake of the house
Of the Lord, our God,
Your welfare
I seek
Each day."

Psalm 123

A song of ascents.

To You
Enthroned in heaven
I raise my eyes;
Like slaves observing
Their masters' hands
For new tasks
That arise;
Or as a maid who,
At a mistress's sign,
Readily complies,
So, to the Lord
Our eyes are raised
Awaiting His favor—
May He be praised.

Show us mercy;
Lord, please do;
For with contempt,
We are shot through.

Long enough
We've been offended
By the scorn that
Smug folk
To us extended;

By the contempt
With which the proud
Are, immeasurably,
Endowed.

Psalm 124

A song of ascents. Of David.

Had the Lord not been
On our side—
Let Israel now say—
Had the Lord not been
On our side
When violent men
Held sway,
They would have swallowed us
Alive;
Their burning rage
None could survive;
Then the waters
Would have carried us off
And the torrent
Swept us away;
The raging waters
Would have covered our heads
Heralding our doomsday.

Blessed be God
Who did not allow us
To be ripped apart
By their teeth;
We were like a bird
Fleeing the fowler's trap
Before it was bolted
Beneath.

Our help is in
The Lord's name;
He made
Heaven and earth
Which we ever acclaim.

Psalm 125

A song of ascents.

Those who believe in the Lord
Like Mount Zion
Are regarded;
They shall not be dislodged;
Forever they're safeguarded.

As Jerusalem
Is enclosed by hills
God enfolds His folk
Forever;
That the scepter of evil
Might not touch the just
Or obstruct
Their best endeavor;
That the righteous
Might not perpetrate
Any crime
Whatsoever.

Grant reward, Lord,
To the good;
To the upright
In heart;
But those who pursue fraudulence
May the Lord set apart
Together with other evildoers—
But to Israel,

Peace
Impart.

Psalm 126

A song of ascents.

As the pilgrims
To Jerusalem
Wended their way
To Zion's center
Here's what they'd say:

"When God restores the fortunes
Of our nation
It will be an undreamed-of
Restoration;
With laughter
Our mouths shall be filled;
Our tongues
With song shall rejoice;
Other nations shall acclaim
The nation of God's choice,
Saying, 'God has done
Wondrous deeds
For a people
Such as these.'"

He has indeed done
Wondrous things;
We are filled with joy
For the blessings
He brings.

Like the driest Negev gullies
Now flooded
With streams,

May our return
Far exceed
All our wildest dreams.

While Zion's farmers
Sowed with tears
Fearing a poor return,
They shall speedily
Reap with cheers
The abundance
They'll discern.

Though he shed many tears
While scattering his meagre seed
He shall rejoice when he turns in
A harvest's bumper yield.

Psalm 127

A song of ascents. Of Solomon.

Unless the Lord
Builds a house
The builders
Labor
In vain;
Unless the Lord
Protects a city
Watchmen
Have nothing
To gain.

Why waste your time
You who rise at dawn
And stay up late
Wholly drawn
Into toiling

For the bread you eat
While His loved ones enjoy
A sleep that's sweet?

Children are a legacy
Bestowed by the Lord;
The fruit of the womb is
His ultimate reward.

As arrows in a warrior's hand
Are those born to one
Still young;
A quiver-full will guarantee
A victory-song
Is sung;
Enemies
That assail their gate,
With little effort
They'll subjugate.

Psalm 128

A song of ascents.

Happy are all
Who fear the Lord;
Who obey
His demands;
Happy are you
And fortunate
To enjoy
The toil of your hands.

Like a fruitful vine
Your wife shall be;
She makes your home
Stable;

Your children
Are like olive shoots
All around
Your table.

The man that truly fears the Lord
Will find blessing in that way;
May He bless you
Out of Zion
That all your days you may
See Jerusalem prosper—
Its success
On display;
Enjoying your children's children—
Peace on Israel
Each day!

Psalm 129

A song of ascents.

Since my youth
They've vexed me,
Let Israel now declare;
Since my youth
They've harassed me,
But never caught me
Unaware.

Across my back
Ploughmen ploughed
And cut lengthy gashes;
The Lord is just,
He snapped the cords
Of the wicked
And soothed their lashes.

Let all who hate Zion
Retreat into disgrace;
Like grass on roofs
That fades before
Being swept up
From its place.

From it
Not a handful
Can the reaper
Collect;
Nor can the sheaf-gatherer retrieve
An armful
To be checked.

There shall be no passerby
With greetings to offer;
No "Blessing of the Lord on you!"
Will they deign
To proffer;
And no response on our part
Shall we readily make;
"We bless you in the Lord's name,"
We shall not undertake.

Psalm 130

A song of ascents.

Lord, I cried out to You
From the depths
Of my despair;
Lord, hear well my voice
And show that You care;
Let Your ears be attentive
To the petition I declare.

If all our sins
You kept on record
That they might survive,
Who could ever cope, Lord,
And who could possibly thrive?

For, forgiveness is yours
To dispense,
That fear of You
May remain intense.

I put my trust in the Lord;
I put my trust in Him;
I waited patiently for His word
Even when times were grim.

I am more eager
For the Lord
Than watchmen
For the dawn,
Or those that hope
Each new day
That they'll be
Reborn.

In God
Let Israel
Fervently hope
For His steadfast love;
And for the great redemptive power
Of the One Above;
Notwithstanding Israel's sins
He'll redeem her,
His dove.

Psalm 131

A song of ascents. Of David.

Lord,
My heart is not proud
Nor haughty are my eyes;
I'll promote no over-ambitious
     schemes
To self-aggrandize.

Rather
I have taught myself
To be content and calm;
Like a babe
On its mother's breast—
God is my soul's
Balm.

Let Israel
Wait for the Lord
From now
And forever
In total accord.

Psalm 132

A song of ascents.

Account to David's merit, Lord,
All his self-denial;
His oath to God—
Jacob's Mighty One—
When He asserted, "I'll
Not enter my home
Nor on my bed lie,
Give to my lids slumber
Or sleep to my eye,

Till I find a place
Where the Lord may reside;
For Jacob's Mighty One
An abode of pride."

Some rumored
The Ark was
In Ephrath;
Others,
In Ja'ar's field;
To the footstool
Of His sanctuary
We shall bow
When it is revealed.

Advance, Lord,
To Your resting-place
You and the Ark of Your might;
Your priests are clothed
In righteousness;
Your pious
Sing with delight.

For the sake of David
Your servant,
Do not reject
Your anointed;
This firm oath
That You won't renounce
You made to the king
You appointed:
"One of your own issue
I will set upon your throne.
If your sons keep
My Covenant
And the decrees
That I made known,

Then their sons also
Until the end of time
Shall occupy your royal seat
With sovereignty sublime."

For God has chosen Zion
As His desired seat;
"This is my abode forever,
It's my preferred retreat;
Its stores of food
I'll amply bless,
With bread
In abundance
For those who have less.

"Its priests
I shall clothe
With salvation,
Its pious shall sing songs
Of celebration.

"There I shall make
David's dynasty thrive;
A lamp to keep the glory
Of my anointed alive.

"I shall clothe his enemies
In disgrace;
While his crown
Shall sparkle
With heavenly grace."

Psalm 133

A song of ascents. To David.

How fine it is
And pleasing
When fellows dwell
As one;
Like goodly oil
Anointing the head
Then flowing down upon
The beard of Aaron
And from there
Continuing to roll on
To anoint the hem
Of his cloak
Like the dew of Mount Hermon;
On Zion's mounts
Duly descending
To receive God's blessing
Of life-unending.

Psalm 134

A song of ascents.

Come bless the Lord
His servants, loyal,
That attend each night
His house;
Lift up Your hands
In holiness;
The Blessing of God
Espouse.

The priest responds:
"May the creator

Of heaven and of earth
Bless you out of Zion—
Unrivalled
In spiritual worth."

Psalm 135

Halleluyah!

Praise God's name
All of you
Servants of the Lord
Who walk the courts
Of the Lord's house
With common accord.

Praise Him for the goodness
That He has dispensed;
Sing your hymns to His name
For its aura
To be sensed.

For God made Jacob
The object of His choice;
Israel, a treasured possession,
Obedient to His voice.
I know
Without a doubt
How great are the Lord's powers;
Above all the so-called
Godly beings
He indubitably towers.

His sovereign will
God calibrates
In heaven
And earth

As He activates;
In seas
And depths
He creates;
Clouds
From earth's end
He transports;
The rain
With lightning
He escorts;
The wind
From its vaults
He imports.

The firstborn of Egypt
He destroyed;
Man and beast
Consigned
To the void;
Signs and wonders
In Egypt
He wrought;
With Pharaoh
And servants
He made sport;
Many nations
He struck down,
Slaying mighty wearers
Of a crown:
Sihon
The Amorite king;
Og of Bashan
Ever battling;
All Canaan's royalty
Took a pounding;
The greatest shock
To all surrounding.

As a heritage
He transferred
To Israel His people—
Much preferred.

Your name will forever
Retain its glory;
Through all generations
Inspiring Israel's story;
For the Lord
Will assuredly
Vindicate His folk;
His servants' sentence
He will revoke.

The nations' idols
Are silver and gold
That men have made
And extolled:
They have
A mouth
But cannot speak;
Eyes
But cannot see;
Ears
They have
But cannot hear;
No breathing
Ability.

Those who make them —
Just like them—
Will become inert;
As will those
That trust in them,
True faith
To subvert.

House of Israel
Bless the Lord;
Aaron's house bless
With one accord.
House of Levi,
Bless the Lord;
God-fearers
Bless Him
And earn reward.

Out of Zion
Bless the Lord
You citizens of
Jerusalem restored.
Halleluyah!—
With faith explored.

Psalm 136

Give thanks to God
For He is good;
His kindness is forever;
To the Supreme God,
The Lord of lords,
The source of all endeavor.
To Him who alone
Has performed
The most wondrous deeds;
For His kindness is eternal—
In abundance it proceeds.

>*His loving-kindness is forever;*
>*He is the source of all endeavor.*

Heaven
In its complexity;
The mighty waters

Of the sea;
The great luminaries
Circulatory;
The sun
That dominates
The day
And the moon and stars
Of the Milky Way.

>*His loving-kindness is forever;*
>*He is the source of all endeavor.*

He smote
The Egyptians;
Their firstborn
Were slain;
Ensuring that they
Were unable to detain
The Hebrew slaves
That became
Their source of pain;
His strong hand
And His out-stretched arm
Delivered Israel
From all harm.

>*His loving-kindness is forever;*
>*He is the source of all endeavor.*

He split the Red Sea
Into corridors
So Israel might reach
The opposite shores;
When Pharaoh and cohorts
Drowned in the Red Sea
Its bluey hue
Soon became bloody.

Through the desert
His folk
He led;
Striking royal tyrants—
Vast numbers dead;
Such as Sihon
The Amorite king
And Og of Bashan
With haughty bearing.

> *His loving-kindness is forever;*
> *He is the source of all endeavor.*

Their lands,
As a heritage
He transferred
To Israel
His servant—
Much preferred.

He remembered us
At our lowliest state;
Saving us from foes
Making hate abate.

> *His loving-kindness is forever;*
> *He is the source of all endeavor.*

To the food provider
For all mankind
Render thanks for all
That He designed.

To the God of heaven
Offer praise,
For His love shall extend
Till the end of days.

Psalm 137

By the rivers of Babylon
We sat down;
Weeping a*nd wearing*
Our deepest frown
When we recalled Zion—
Our former crown.

On its poplar trees
Our harps
We hung
When our captors demanded
That our songs
Be sung;
The tormentors wished
To be entertained:
"Sing your songs of Zion!"—
But we refrained!
How could we sing
The Lord's song
In a foreign land—
It felt so wrong!

If I forget you
Jerusalem
Let my right hand's strength
Fail;
Let my tongue stick
To my palate
If remembrance
Won't prevail;
If, at the pinnacle of my joy,
Jerusalem
I don't hail.

Remember, Lord,

The Edomites
On the day of
Jerusalem's fall;
Constantly baying
To strip her down
To the foundation
Of every wall.

O daughter
Of Babylon,
You are fated
To be laid waste;
How happy the one
Who shall make you pay
For rendering us
Debased.

Happy shall be
The one to seize
Your infants
And smash their heads
Against your country's
Rocky crags
As retribution
Spreads.

Psalm 138

Of David

I shall praise You
With all my heart;
Before the nations' gods
I'll set You apart.

Bowing toward

Your sacred Temple
I shall praise Your name;
Your mercy
And Your truth unending
I shall proclaim;
For the exaltedness
Of Your being
Exceeds what men acclaim.

I merely
Had to utter the plea
And Your response
Was made;
You gave me pride in myself
And the strength
To make the grade.

All earth's kings
Shall praise You
When they hear
The words of Your lips;
They shall sing paeans
Praising God's ways
For His glory
All else outstrips

Exalted
Though the Lord is,
For the lowly
He cares;
The haughty
From a distance
Are caught
Unawares.

If I found myself trapped

In trouble's web
You'd preserve my life,
You wouldn't
Let it ebb;
You would extend Your hand
To stifle
My foes' ire;
You'd save me
With Your right-hand
From dangers
Most dire.

Lord, You'll settle
My every score;
Your mercy forever
Shall reassure;
Your handiwork
Do not abjure.

Psalm 139

For the Director.
Of David. A psalm.

Lord, You've scrutinized me;
All my thoughts
You know;
Whether I choose
To sit or to stand
Your Will
I echo.
Whether walking
Or reclining
All my motives
You're divining;
All my ways
You're analyzing.

Even before any words
Are able to escape my lips
You know every one of them—
Down to
The smallest quips.

You envelop me
Behind and before;
With Your guiding hand
I feel secure.

The extent of Your knowledge
I cannot comprehend;
To grasp its uniqueness
I cannot pretend.

From Your Spirit
Where might I flee?
From Your probing Presence
Could I ever break free?

Were I to scale
The heavens
I would find You
There;
Were I to bed down
In the grave
Of You
I'd be aware.

If I spread my wings
To greet the dawn
Or plumbed
The depths of the sea,
Even there
Your hand would reach;
Your right hand

Would grasp me.

If I thought that darkness
might conceal me
From Your sight,
I should know
In night's darkest hour
I'd be in Your spotlight;
For darkness
Cannot provide for me
Concealment
From You;
For in the night
As in the day
All is within Your view;
Both in the dark
As in the light
You readily
See through.

You were the One
Who gave me form
And designed my essence;
In my mother's womb
You knit me into
A physical presence.

It calls for praise
That I am made
Of such complexity;
All Your deeds
Are awesome—
They overwhelm me!

Not so much as a single limb
Escapes Your attention;

In the womb's recess
You melded me
Safe from intervention.

You viewed me
As a formless being
As part of
Your detailed plan
For how the limbs
Of all on earth
Would take the form
Of man.

How overawed
I am, Lord,
By Your thoughts
Sublime;
And how innumerable
They are—
They span
The whole of time.

Had I thought
To count them—
They exceed
The grains of sand;
I'd wake each day
Still thinking of You
And what for me
You've planned.

If the wicked, Lord,
You would but slay,
And keep the blood-thirsty
At bay—
Those who address You
While speaking guile;

Lying foes
Whom You revile.

Those who hate You,
Lord, I hate;
Your adversaries
I denigrate;
I hate them
With a hate
Intense;
Bitter foes
Becoming
In consequence.

Probe me, Lord,
And know my mind;
Test me
And my thoughts
Unwind.

See if I've brought
On myself grief
And lead me to
Everlasting relief.

Psalm 140

For the Director.
A psalm of David.

Rescue me, Lord,
From an evil man;
Keep me safe
From the violent
And their clan
That devise evil
In their mind,

Each day brewing battles
Of every kind;
Sharpening their tongues
Like serpents do;
On their lips
The poison
That asps spew.

So, save me from the hands
Of an evil man;
Keep me safe
From the violent
And their clan;
For whom my downfall
Is their chief plan.

Arrogant men
Have laid their snare;
Ropes at the ready
To catch me
Unaware;
Spreading their nets
Along my route
Setting traps—
In hot pursuit.

I said to God:
"You are my Lord;
Attending whenever
I implored;
You, whose strength
Is my salvation
Have protected my head
Throughout wars'
Duration.

The desires

Of the wicked
Do not fulfil;
Their intrigue
Bring to a stand-still;
Lest they think of themselves
As invincible.

Let instigators
Of the ambush
Which for me
Was laid
With the venom
Of their own tongues
Be amply repaid.

Let red-hot coals
On them
Be poured;
Into furnaces
Let them be lured;
With no escape
Ever secured.

Let the slanderers
Have no place
In the land
Blessed
By Your grace;
Root out the evil
Of men of violence;
Sentence them
To eternal silence.

I know
The Lord will champion
The cause of
The poor;

The right of the needy
He'll pursue
For evermore.

The righteous will assuredly
Acknowledge Your name;
To witness Your Presence
The upright shall lay claim.

Psalm 141

A psalm of David.

Lord
When I call on You
Hurry to my aid;
Attend to all the things
For which
I have prayed.

Consider my prayer worthy
As the incense
Offered;
As the evening sacrifice
My own hands have proffered.

Guard my mouth
And suppress
Any unworthy remark;
Against an evil utterance
Make my lips a bulwark.

With evil-doers
Let me not feast;
Nor enjoy their delicacies
In the least.

If a righteous man strikes me
It's a benign reproof;
From an oil as choice as that
Let me not remain aloof.

To resist evil-doers' harm
Is my petition;
Let their leaders
Be hurled down a cliff
Into perdition;
But, better,
Let my words inspire
Their immediate contrition.

Through them,
At the mouth of Sheol
Our bones are scattered;
Like earth ground up
Into lumps
They shall all be splattered.

Hence my eyes, trustingly,
Are raised to You;
Do not leave me exposed,
But come to my rescue;
Save me from the trap
They have laid for me;
From evil-doers
And their jeopardy.

Let the wicked fall
Into their own nets,
But endow me with the courage
To brush aside their threats.

Psalm 142

A maskil of David, recited when
he was in the cave. A prayer.

To God
I cry
With anguished shout;
Petitioning Him
As I cry out.

Before Him
I present
My complaint;
Relating my troubles
Without restraint;
I sense that I am
Ready to faint;
You know where I'm heading—
You know my fate.

In the same direction
That I go
Traps have been laid
By my foe;
When, in hope,
I look to the right
Not a single friend
Appears in sight;
There is no option
Offered by flight
For there is no one
To consider my plight.

Hence my cry
To You, Lord,
In the hope that
Refuge

You'll afford,
And my portion
You'll secure
In the land of the living
Among the pure.

I appeal to You,
To my cry
Attend
For I am low—
And at my wits' end.

From my pursuers
Save me, please;
Their strength
Has brought me
To my knees!

I beg You
Release me
From my jail,
That, Your name,
I might hail;
That the righteous
May be crowned
Reward for Your favor
That I've found.

Psalm 143

A psalm of David.

Lord, I beg You,
Hear my prayer;
Of my petition
Be aware;
In faith and righteousness

Attend,
To bring my woes
To their end.

Don't summon me to appear
Before Your highest court;
Man's vindication
On Your part
Is rarely ever wrought.

The enemy is
In hot pursuit,
My spirit is crushed
By dread;
They housed me
In dark places
Like those
Long-since dead.

My spirit
Within me
Evaporates;
My heart
Through shock
Palpitates;
Then I recalled
The by-gone days
When I would marvel
At Your ways,
And recount
All Your deeds
How You supplied
All my needs.

I lifted up my hands
To You
In earnest petition;

Thirsting as parched land does
For its dewy nutrition.

Answer me speedily
For my spirit
Is dejected;
Hide not Your Face
That I don't become
Like those
To the pit,
Rejected.

Of Your kindness,
Each morning
Make me aware;
For in You I put my trust
Knowing that You care.

Show me the way
I should face
For my soul yearns
For Your embrace.

Save me, Lord,
From foes all around;
Grant me the concealment
That with You
Is found.

Teach me
That I might fulfil
Whatever accords
With Your Will;
For You are my God,
And Your spirit
So pure
Will guide me along

The path
Most secure.

For Your name's sake,
Let my spirit
Revive;
By Your Grace,
All trouble
Let me survive;
In Your infinite kindness
My foes
You'll destroy;
Those that
Harassment
Ever employ;
That I,
Your servant,
Might serve You
With joy.

Psalm 144

Of David

Blessed be the Lord, my rock,
Determined to train
My hands to fight battles
And my fingers
To take aim.

He shows me
Loving-kindness;
He's my fortress
And my tower;
Deliverer, shield,
And refuge;
Over peoples

Giving me
Power.

Wherein does man merit
To receive Your attention,
Or the son of man
That he invites
Your consideration?

Man is just as a breath—
So transient is he;
His days pass
As a shadow
With rapidity.

Lord,
Bend Your heavens
That You may descend;
You just touch the mountains
To make their smoke ascend.

With a flash
Of lightning
Scatter
My foes;
Mortify them
When You discharge
Your deadly arrows;
Stretch forth
Your hands
From on high
To save me from storms
That rage to the sky;
From alien foes
Who,
Truth
Deny;

Lifting their right hands—
Each oath
A lie.

To you, Lord,
I shall sing
A new song;
With a ten-stringed harp
To You I'll sing along.

Victory to kings
You accord;
Saving David Your servant
From the deadly sword.

Rescue and deliver me
From the hand of alien foes;
Lying mouths
With right hands raised
To utter
Their false oaths.

Make our sons
Like rooted plants,
In youth
Sturdily formed;
Our daughters
Like carved corner-stones
Of palaces,
Well adorned.

Our stores
Are all fully stocked;
All kinds of food
They yield;
By a thousand
And ten thousand times,

Sheep increase
In the field;
Our oxen
Bear their heavy loads
Of produce
On our nation's roads;
No breaches in our walls
Are found,
No fugitives
Go to ground;
In our streets
No mourning sound.

Happy the nation
That all this
Can boast;
Happy those whose God
Is the Lord of Hosts.

Psalm 145

A song of praise. Of David.

My God and king
I'll hail You
And forever
Bless Your name;
Each day
To offer blessing
Shall be my highest aim;
Indeed, for an eternity
To do the very same.

Great is the Lord
And most worthy of praise;
Unfathomable
Is His greatness—

Hence the awe
That man displays.

One generation
To the next,
Your deeds
describe;
The mighty acts
That You perform
Each one
Shall imbibe.

The glory
Of Your majesty;
Your splendor
Beyond compare;
The details
Of Your wonders—
All of them
I declare.

The power
Of those wonders
People shall extol;
And I shall eagerly relate
The greatness
Of Your role.

Your abundant goodness
Men shall celebrate;
And of Your generosity
They'll sing
And narrate.

Gracious and merciful
Is the Lord;
Patient and generous

In the kindness
He'll accord.

The Lord's bounty
He extends to all;
His mercies
Hold all mankind
In their thrall.

Lord,
All Your works
Acclaim You;
All Your pious
Praise You;
Your glorious kingdom
They affirm;
Your greatness
They all confirm.

They reinforce
To all mankind
The nature of His might,
And His majestic glory
In which they all delight.

Your kingdom shall extend
To all eternity;
Your dominion
Over every age,
Triumphantly.

The Lord supports
All who fall;
Those cowed with care
Again walk tall.

The eyes of all
Are raised to You
In anticipation,
That You'll provide
The food
They need
And banish starvation.

You open Your hand
And favor
All who are in need;
You are righteous in all You do
And faithful
In every deed.

God is near
To all who call
On Him
In their plight;
All who call
Whole-heartedly
He has
In His sight.

To the wishes
Of all who fear Him
He closely attends;
He hears their cries considerately,
And deliverance
Promptly sends.

The Lord protects all those
Whose love is sincere;
But to their destruction
The wicked
He will steer.

Praise of the Lord
My mouth shall frame;
Let all humankind forever
Bless His holy name.

Psalm 146

Halleluyah!

My fervent wish
O my soul
Is that praise of God
Will be your goal.

While I live
Let me offer praise
And sing to God
Throughout my days.

Let not your trust
In princes, be;
Mere men—
They offer no victory.

When their breath expires,
To earth they return;
End of all the grand plans
That were their prime concern.

But happy is he
Who seeks the aid
Of Jacob's God—
And is not afraid;
In the Lord lies
His expectation,
For He oversaw

The formation
Of heaven and earth
And life in the sea,
And keeps faith with it all
Wholeheartedly.

For the oppressed
He seeks redress;
Providing the hungry
With bread
To bless;
Freeing those
Under arrest.

Those who walk heedlessly
He enables
To see;
Those who are bowed low with care
He renders
Carefree;
He loves the righteous
Unconditionally.

To strangers He offers
His protection;
To orphans and widows
Support;
But the path
That the wicked choose
He will consistently distort.

The Lord shall rule
Forever;
As your God, Zion,
He'll reign;
Throughout the generations,

Halleluyah!
Is the acclaim.

Psalm 147

Halleluyah!
It is truly good
To praise our God on high;
It is pleasant and most beautiful
To praise Him
To the sky.

The Lord rebuilds
Jerusalem;
Israel's scattered
All in-gathered;
He heals the broken-hearted
And bandages
The battered.

He counts the stars
By number
And gives them all
Their names;
Supreme
Is He
In greatness;
His power
Never wanes;
Infinite is the wisdom
That He displays;
It defies the vocabulary
Of human praise.
Humble folk
The Lord upholds;
The wicked

To earth
Consigned;
So, sing to the Lord
With thanksgiving;
Sing praise
With harp
Assigned.

The heavens
With His clouds
He shields;
Ample rain
For earth
He yields;
The mountains
Sprouting grass
Like fields.

On Him,
The beast
For food
Relies;
Young ravens call—
And He supplies.

In a horse's strength
He takes no delight,
Nor in man's thigh muscles
However tight;
His pleasure is in those
Who display awe;
Who by His mercy,
Put great store.

Glorify the Lord
O Jerusalem;
Let your God,

O Zion,
Be praised;
For He made secure
The bars of your gates
And blessed children there
That you raised.

He ensures your borders
Are peaceful
And you're nourished
With choicest wheat;
His Word
He transmits
Throughout the earth
With a speed
None can repeat.

He sends snow
As white as wool;
He makes hoar-frost
Like ashes
Disperse;
Hail
Like crumbs
He casts down;
To His cold
Who is not
Averse?

A further command—
And they melt;
At His breath
Water flows
And is forcefully felt.

Those commands,
As given to Jacob,

To Israel
As statute and law,
To no other nation
Did He reveal—
Higher justice
Is at their core.

Halleluyah!
Praise the Lord;
All His deeds
We applaud.

Psalm 148

Halleluyah!

Praise God
From the heavens;
Praise Him
From the height;
Praise Him
All His messengers—
Agents of
His might.

Praise Him
O sun and moon
And all you
Stellar lights;
Praise Him highest heavens
And the waters
Above their heights.

To the Lord's name
Let them offer praise;
When He commands
Creation obeys.

He established them
That they might last
For an eternity;
Governed by
The immutable laws
Of His divine
Decree.

Praise the Lord
From the earth
O monsters of the sea;
Inhabitants of
The lowest depths,
Enjoying their marine spree.

Fire and hail
Snow and mist
Storm wind
Doing as told;
Mountains, hills,
Fruit-giving trees
And cedars
Centuries old;
Beasts and cattle
Creeping things
Birds in flight
And earthly kings;
All the peoples
And their leaders
Nations' judges
And court pleaders;
Boys and girls
Old and young—
All of you
Praise God's name;
Praise Him on Earth
And in heaven;

Unique
Is His fame.

To His people
His glory is granted;
To all His pious,
Praise;
O Israel
His closest ones
A *Halleluyah!*
Raise.

Psalm 149

Halleluyah!

Praise the Lord
And to Him
A new song
Sing;
In the assembly
Of the saints
Let the sound of His praise
Ring.

Let Israel's joy
In its Maker
Ever abound;
Let Zion's offspring's
Joy in their king
Ever be profound.

With dancing
Let them praise
His name;
With tambourine and harp
Voice their acclaim.

For the Lord delights
In His nation;
Adorning the humble
With salvation.

In the gift of His glory
Let the pious rejoice;
On their beds
Let them sing
With full voice.

Out of their mouths
They offer to God
Ecstatic exultation;
Armed
With double-edged swords
Readied for confrontation;
To wreak vengeance
On the nations;
On peoples
Countless rebukes;
Binding with chains
All their kings,
With iron cuffs
Their dukes;
In confirmation
Of the sentence
Foretold in Holy Writ:
Satisfaction
For the pious—
Halleluyah!
Their remit.

Psalm 150

Halleluyah!

Praise God in His sanctuary
In the firmament of His power;
Praise Him for His unique deeds
For being our rock and tower;
Praise Him with trumpet sound
With harp and lyre;
Praise Him with timbrel
With dance *and choir;*
Praise Him with strings and flute
With cymbals clashing loud;
With all means of percussion
Amid the assembled crowd.

Let all who breathe
Praise the Lord!
Affirming how much
He is adored.

11494842R00136

Printed in Great Britain
by Amazon